TABLE OF CONTENTS

THE DIABETIC TYPE 2 DIET

UNDERSTANDING TYPE 2 DIABETES AND NUTRITION

THE POWER OF QUICK, HEALTHY MEALS

INGREDIENTS TO EMBRACE AND AVOID

MASTERING THE ART OF SUBSTITUTION   6

BREAKFASTS TO START YOUR DAY

GREEK YOGURT WITH MIXED BERRIES AND FLAXSEEDS	7
AVOCADO TOAST ON WHOLE GRAIN BREAD	8
SCRAMBLED EGGS WITH SPINACH AND FETA	9
ALMOND BUTTER AND BANANA SMOOTHIE	10
COTTAGE CHEESE WITH PINEAPPLE CHUNKS	11
QUICK OATS WITH ALMOND MILK AND CHIA SEEDS	12
SMOKED SALMON AND CREAM CHEESE CUCUMBER BITES	13
BERRY AND NUT YOGURT PARFAIT	14

SATISFYING SNACKS

APPLE SLICES WITH PEANUT BUTTER	15
CARROT AND CUCUMBER STICKS WITH HUMMUS	16
MIXED NUTS AND DRIED FRUIT TRAIL MIX	17
RICOTTA AND BERRY WHOLE WHEAT CRACKERS	18
TURKEY AND CHEESE ROLL-UPS	19
CHERRY TOMATOES WITH MOZZARELLA BALLS AND BASIL	20

LIGHT LUNCHES

TUNA SALAD ON MIXED GREENS	21
CHICKEN CAESAR SALAD WRAP	22
SMOKED SALMON AND AVOCADO SALAD	23
QUINOA SALAD WITH CUCUMBERS AND FETA	24
TURKEY BREAST AND AVOCADO LETTUCE WRAPS	25
GREEK SALAD WITH OLIVES AND FETA CHEESE	26
CAPRESE SALAD WITH BALSAMIC GLAZE	27
EGG SALAD ON WHOLE GRAIN TOAST	28
SPINACH AND GOAT CHEESE STUFFED PORTOBELLO MUSHROOM	29
SHRIMP AND AVOCADO TACO SALAD	30

HEARTY DINNERS

GARLIC LEMON SHRIMP OVER ZUCCHINI NOODLES	31
QUICK BEEF STIR-FRY WITH BELL PEPPERS	32
PAN-SEARED SALMON WITH SPINACH SALAD	33
CHICKEN FAJITAS WITH PRE-CUT VEGGIES	34
TOFU AND VEGETABLE STIR-FRY WITH SOY SAUCE	35
SPAGHETTI SQUASH WITH MARINARA SAUCE (MICROWAVE COOKED)	36
GRILLED CHICKEN BREAST WITH STEAMED BROCCOLI	37
PORK TENDERLOIN MEDALLIONS WITH APPLE SLAW	38
BALSAMIC GLAZED STEAK BITES AND TOMATOES	39
CAULIFLOWER FRIED RICE WITH EGG AND PEAS	40

TABLE OF CONTENTS

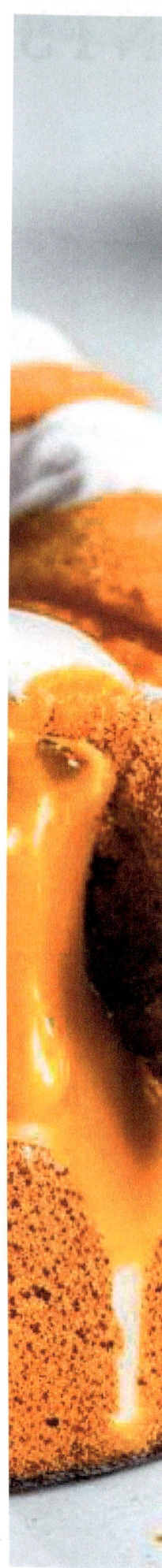

VEGETARIAN AND VEGAN DELIGHTS

AVOCADO AND BLACK BEAN SALAD	41
VEGAN TACOS WITH REFRIED BEANS AND AVOCADO	42
SPICY CHICKPEA LETTUCE WRAPS	43
QUICK VEGGIE AND HUMMUS SANDWICH	44
ZUCCHINI AND CORN SAUTÉ WITH BASIL	45
VEGAN PESTO AND TOMATO TOAST	46
SPINACH AND MUSHROOM QUESADILLAS	47
EDAMAME SALAD WITH SESAME GINGER DRESSING	48

SIDE DISHES TO COMPLEMENT

STEAMED GREEN BEANS WITH LEMON ZEST	49
QUICK PICKLED CUCUMBER SALAD	50
SAUTÉED KALE WITH GARLIC AND OLIVE OIL	51
MICROWAVE STEAMED ASPARAGUS	52
TOMATO AND ONION SALAD WITH OLIVE OIL	53
ROASTED RED PEPPER AND WALNUT DIP	54
SWEET CORN AND BLACK BEAN SALAD	55
GARLIC AND HERB MICROWAVE-STEAMED CARROTS	56

SOUPS AND STEWS

QUICK TOMATO BASIL SOUP	57
SIMPLE MISO SOUP	58
MINI FRITTATAS WITH SPINACH AND FETA	59
ZUCCHINI AND BASIL SOUP	60
PEA AND MINT SOUP	61
SPICY BLACK BEAN SOUP	62
SHRIMP CORN SOUP	63

DESSERTS

GREEK YOGURT WITH HONEY AND CINNAMON	64
DARK CHOCOLATE-DIPPED STRAWBERRIES	65
RICOTTA AND HONEY WITH SLICED ALMONDS	66
FRESH FRUIT SALAD WITH MINT	67
FROZEN BLUEBERRIES WITH A DRIZZLE OF CREAM	68
MANGO AND COCONUT RICE PAPER ROLLS	69
AVOCADO CHOCOLATE MOUSSE	70

60-DAY MEAL PLAN   71

Understanding Type 2 Diabetes and Nutrition

Type 2 Diabetes is a chronic condition that affects the way the body metabolizes glucose, an essential source of energy derived from food, particularly carbohydrates. In Type 2 Diabetes, the body either resists the effects of insulin — a hormone that regulates the movement of sugar into your cells — or doesn't produce enough insulin to maintain normal glucose levels. This resistance or deficiency leads to elevated levels of glucose in the blood, which can have long-term detrimental effects on various organs and systems if not managed effectively.

The Role of Nutrition
Nutrition plays a pivotal role in managing Type 2 Diabetes. A well-considered diet can help maintain blood glucose levels within a target range, thereby reducing the risk of complications such as heart disease, kidney failure, and nerve damage. The key is to focus on whole, nutrient-dense foods that provide essential vitamins, minerals, and fiber, while minimizing processed foods high in sugar and unhealthy fats.

Carbohydrates and Glycemic Index
Understanding carbohydrates is crucial for managing diabetes. Carbohydrates are found in foods like fruits, vegetables, grains, and dairy products and are the body's main energy source. However, not all carbs are created equal. The Glycemic Index (GI) is a useful tool for choosing carbohydrates wisely. It ranks carbohydrates on a scale from 0 to 100 based on how quickly they raise blood sugar levels after eating. Foods with a low GI (55 or less) are absorbed more slowly, causing a gradual rise in blood sugar levels, which is beneficial for diabetes management.

Fiber-Rich Foods
Fiber plays a significant role in diabetes management. High-fiber foods not only help slow the absorption of sugar, but they also contribute to feelings of fullness, aiding in weight management — a crucial aspect for many individuals with Type 2 Diabetes. Foods rich in fiber include vegetables, fruits, legumes, and whole grains.

Healthy Fats
Incorporating healthy fats into the diet can also have positive effects on heart health, which is important since diabetes increases the risk of heart disease. Sources of healthy fats include avocados, nuts, seeds, and olive oil. These fats can help lower bad cholesterol levels and reduce inflammation.

Protein
Protein is essential for repairing cells and creating new ones. It's especially important for individuals with Type 2 Diabetes to include a moderate amount of protein in their diet, as it has minimal impact on blood sugar levels. Good sources of protein include lean meats, fish, poultry, legumes, and dairy products.

The Importance of Meal Planning
Meal planning is a vital strategy in managing Type 2 Diabetes. It involves balancing the right amount of carbohydrates, proteins, and fats to maintain stable blood glucose levels throughout the day. Planning meals can also help avoid the temptation of unhealthy food choices, which is crucial for maintaining overall health and well-being. Understanding Type 2 Diabetes and the pivotal role of nutrition in its management is the first step toward living a healthier life. By focusing on nutrient-dense foods, paying attention to the glycemic index, and incorporating a variety of food groups into your diet, you can take control of your diabetes and enjoy a wide range of delicious meals without spending hours in the kitchen. This cookbook aims to empower you with the knowledge and recipes needed to manage your condition effectively, proving that a diabetes-friendly diet can be both nutritious and delightful.

The Power of Quick, Healthy Meals

The Link Between Diet and Diabetes Management
Type 2 Diabetes is a condition characterized by insulin resistance, where the body's cells do not respond effectively to insulin, leading to elevated blood sugar levels. Diet plays a crucial role in managing this condition, as the types and amounts of food consumed directly impact blood sugar levels. A balanced diet rich in nutrients, fiber, and healthy fats, along with controlled portions of carbohydrates, can aid in blood sugar regulation, weight management, and the reduction of diabetes-related complications.

The Challenges of Traditional Meal Preparation
Traditional meal preparation often conjures images of time-consuming cooking processes and complex recipes. For many living with Type 2 Diabetes, this can seem daunting, especially when balancing the demands of daily life. The misconception that healthy eating requires extensive preparation time can discourage individuals from pursuing a diet that could significantly improve their health and quality of life.

Embracing Quick, Healthy Meals
The concept of quick, healthy meals is a game-changer for diabetes management. These meals are not only simple and fast to prepare but are also designed to meet nutritional guidelines that support blood sugar control and overall health. Embracing this approach can help mitigate the stress of meal planning and preparation, making it more feasible to maintain a healthy diet amidst a busy lifestyle.

Benefits of Quick, Healthy Meals
- **Time Efficiency**: Quick meals require shorter preparation and cooking times, freeing up valuable time for other activities or rest.
- **Simplicity**: Simplified recipes with fewer ingredients can reduce the complexity of cooking, making it more accessible to everyone, regardless of their culinary skills.
- **Nutritional Value**: Quick meals do not compromise on nutrition; they can be rich in vitamins, minerals, and fiber, which are essential for managing Type 2 Diabetes.
- **Portion Control**: Easy-to-prepare meals can help with portion control, an important aspect of diabetes management.

Key Ingredients for Quick, Healthy Meals
Focusing on certain ingredients can streamline the cooking process while ensuring nutritional needs are met. These include:
- **Lean Proteins**: Chicken breast, turkey, fish, tofu, and legumes can be prepared quickly and are great sources of protein.
- **Whole Grains**: Quinoa, brown rice, and whole grain pastas are not only nutritious but also easy to cook in bulk for multiple meals.
- **Fresh Vegetables**: A variety of colorful vegetables can be quickly steamed, sautéed, or eaten raw, providing essential nutrients and fiber.
- **Healthy Fats**: Avocado, nuts, seeds, and olive oil add flavor and heart-healthy fats to meals without requiring extensive preparation.

Strategies for Quick, Healthy Cooking
Adopting certain strategies can make the preparation of quick, healthy meals even easier:
- **Meal Planning**: Spend a few minutes each week planning meals. This can help streamline grocery shopping and reduce decision fatigue during the week.
- **Batch Cooking**: Preparing ingredients or entire meals in advance can save time. Cooked grains, proteins, and chopped vegetables can be refrigerated or frozen for later use.
- **Simple Cooking Methods**: Grilling, broiling, steaming, and stir-frying are quick cooking methods that retain the nutritional value of foods.
- **Healthy Shortcuts**: Utilize healthy pre-prepared ingredients, such as pre-washed greens, canned beans, or frozen vegetables to cut down on prep time.

Ingredients to Embrace and Avoid

Navigating nutrition for Type 2 Diabetes management involves a careful selection of foods to embrace for their beneficial properties, as well as those to avoid due to their potential negative impact on blood sugar levels and overall health. Key to this approach is understanding the nutritional value of different ingredients and how they fit into a diabetes-friendly diet.

Foods rich in fiber, such as leafy greens, berries, nuts, seeds, legumes, and whole grains like oats and barley, are essential. Fiber slows the absorption of sugar into the bloodstream, helping to moderate blood glucose levels and promote satiety, which is crucial for weight management. Equally important are healthy fats found in avocados, olives, nuts, seeds, and fatty fish like salmon and mackerel. These fats improve insulin sensitivity and lower the risk of heart disease, which individuals with Type 2 Diabetes are more prone to.

Lean proteins, including chicken breast, turkey, fish, tofu, legumes, and eggs, support metabolic health and maintain muscle mass without significantly impacting blood glucose. Low-Glycemic Index (GI) carbohydrates, such as sweet potatoes, quinoa, lentils, and non-starchy vegetables, offer a slower, more controlled release of glucose into the bloodstream. Antioxidant-rich foods like dark chocolate, blueberries, spinach, and nuts fight inflammation and oxidative stress, reducing the risk of diabetes complications.

On the flip side, certain ingredients can exacerbate blood sugar fluctuations and contribute to health issues. Refined carbohydrates, found in white bread, pastries, and white rice, are quickly absorbed and spike blood sugar levels. Added sugars in sugar-sweetened beverages and sweets lead to weight gain and an increased risk of heart disease. Trans fats, present in margarine, fried foods, and processed snacks, harm insulin sensitivity and heart health. High sodium foods raise blood pressure, a significant concern for those with diabetes. High-GI carbohydrates, like baked potatoes and short-grain white rice, cause rapid increases in blood glucose and should be consumed sparingly.

Incorporating the right ingredients into your diet doesn't have to be a daunting task. Meal planning and reading food labels can help you make informed decisions, ensuring a varied and nutritionally balanced diet. Experimenting with healthier substitutes, such as using whole grain instead of white pasta or adding cinnamon for sweetness, can make meals enjoyable and diabetes-friendly. Cooking at home allows for better control over ingredients, helping to avoid unhealthy options prevalent in processed and fast foods.

Mindful eating practices, focusing on hunger and fullness cues and savoring the eating experience, can further support diabetes management. This approach encourages moderation and thoughtful food choices, enhancing the effectiveness of a diabetes-friendly diet.

Mastering the Art of Substitution

Understanding the Need for Substitutions
The foods we eat directly impact our blood sugar levels, and for individuals managing type 2 diabetes, maintaining stable glucose readings is paramount. Traditional recipes often call for ingredients that can spike blood sugar, such as refined sugars, white flour, and certain fats. However, with a few smart swaps, these dishes can be transformed into nutritious, diabetes-friendly versions that are just as satisfying.

Sweeteners: Rethinking Sugar
Refined sugar is a common ingredient in desserts and sweet dishes but can lead to blood sugar spikes. Natural sweeteners offer a better alternative, providing the sweetness you crave with a lower impact on glucose levels. Consider options like:
- **Stevia**: A zero-calorie plant-based sweetener that doesn't raise blood sugar.
- **Erythritol**: A sugar alcohol with minimal calories that's suitable for baking.
- **Monk Fruit Sweetener**: Known for its no-calorie sweetness without affecting blood sugar.

When using these sweeteners, start with small amounts and adjust according to taste, as their sweetness can be more intense than sugar.

Flour: Going Beyond White
White flour is a staple in baking and cooking but lacks nutritional value and can affect blood glucose. Whole grain and nut flours are excellent substitutes, offering more fiber, vitamins, and minerals:
- **Almond Flour**: Great for baking, almond flour adds a nutty flavor and is low in carbs.
- **Coconut Flour**: Highly absorbent and rich in fiber, it's perfect for cakes and bread.
- **Whole Wheat Flour**: For a direct substitution, whole wheat flour provides more nutrients than white flour.

Substituting flours may require adjusting liquid ratios in recipes, as whole grain and nut flours have different absorption levels.

Fats: Choosing Healthier Options
Fats play a crucial role in cooking, adding flavor and texture. However, not all fats are created equal:
- **Olive Oil**: A heart-healthy monounsaturated fat ideal for dressings and sautéing.
- **Avocado Oil**: With a high smoke point, it's suitable for high-heat cooking.
- **Coconut Oil**: Rich in medium-chain triglycerides, it's a good option for baking.

Replacing saturated fats with these healthier fats can enhance your diet's nutritional profile without sacrificing the dishes' richness.

Dairy: Low-Fat and Plant-Based Alternatives
Dairy products add creaminess to recipes but can be high in fat and sugar. Low-fat and plant-based alternatives provide similar textures with fewer calories and carbs:
- **Greek Yogurt**: Use in place of sour cream or mayonnaise for a protein-rich option.
- **Almond Milk**: A versatile, low-calorie substitute for cow's milk in many recipes.
- **Cashew Cheese**: A creamy, dairy-free alternative for cheese in sauces and spreads.

Vegetables: Increasing Fiber and Nutrients
Incorporating more vegetables into your meals is a fantastic way to increase fiber, vitamins, and minerals while keeping carbs in check:
- **Zucchini Noodles**: Replace pasta with "zoodles" for a low-carb, nutrient-packed dish.
- **Cauliflower Rice**: A versatile substitute for white rice that's lower in calories and carbs.
- **Leafy Greens**: Swap tortillas for lettuce wraps to reduce carbs and add crunch.

Greek Yogurt with Mixed Berries and Flaxseeds

1. **Gather Ingredients (1 minute)** Gather all the ingredients listed above. Make sure the Greek yogurt is chilled and the berries are washed. This simple step lays the foundation for a quick and efficient assembly of your healthy breakfast. Keeping ingredients prepared and accessible streamlines the cooking process, ensuring a smooth start.
2. **Prepare the Berries (2 minutes)** Wash and prepare the mixed berries. If using strawberries, hull and halve them to match the size of the blueberries and raspberries. This step is crucial for ensuring all components of the dish blend well together, both in taste and in presentation, making every spoonful delightfully balanced.
3. **Add Yogurt to Plate (2 minutes)** Spoon the Greek yogurt onto a plate. Spread it out lightly with the back of the spoon to create a smooth, even base. The creamy texture of the yogurt serves as the perfect canvas for the vibrant berries and the nutty crunch of the flaxseeds, promising a medley of textures.
4. **Top with Berries and Flaxseeds (4 minutes)** Arrange the mixed berries over the yogurt. Sprinkle the flaxseeds evenly on top. The bright colors of the berries contrast beautifully against the yogurt, while the flaxseeds add a subtle crunch and a boost of nutrition, including Omega-3 fatty acids, which are beneficial for managing Type 2 diabetes.
5. **Serve Immediately (1 minute)** Your Greek Yogurt with Mixed Berries and Flaxseeds is ready to enjoy. This final step presents the dish in its full glory, ready to be savored. The quick preparation time ensures that every bite is as fresh as possible, maximizing both flavor and nutritional benefits.

INGREDIENTS

- 1 cup (240g) Greek yogurt
- 1/2 cup (70g) mixed berries (strawberries, blueberries, raspberries)
- 1 tablespoon (10g) flaxseeds

NUTRITION

- **Kcal per serve:** 150 kcal
- **Carbohydrates:** 18g
- **Sugars:** 12g
- **Fiber:** 4g
- **Protein:** 20g
- **Total Fats:** 4g
- **Saturated Fats:** 1g
- **Monounsaturated Fats:** 1g
- **Polyunsaturated Fats:** 2g
- **Sodium:** 60mg

Avocado Toast on Whole Grain Bread

1. **Toast the Bread (2 minutes)** Toast the whole grain bread slices to your preferred level of crunchiness. Whole grain bread is chosen for its low glycemic index, which is beneficial for blood sugar control in Type 2 diabetes.
2. **Prepare the Avocado (3 minutes)** While the bread is toasting, halve the avocado, remove the pit, and scoop the flesh into a bowl. Add lemon juice, salt, and pepper, then mash to a creamy consistency. Lemon adds freshness and helps prevent oxidation.
3. **Spread Avocado on Toast (2 minutes)** Evenly spread the mashed avocado over each slice of toasted bread. The creaminess of the avocado contrasts perfectly with the crunch of the toast, providing a satisfying texture and rich flavor.
4. **Garnish (2 minutes)** Sprinkle chia seeds over the avocado toast for an extra nutritional boost, including omega-3 fatty acids, which are beneficial for heart health—a concern for those with Type 2 diabetes.
5. **Serve (1 minute)** Serve the avocado toast immediately to enjoy its freshness and flavors at their peak. This quick and nutritious meal is perfect for a diabetes-friendly diet, offering a balance of healthy fats, fiber, and protein.

INGREDIENTS

- 2 slices whole grain bread (approx. 70g per slice)
- 1 medium avocado (about 200g)
- 1/2 teaspoon (2.5g) lemon juice
- Pinch of salt (less than 1g)
- Pinch of black pepper (less than 1g)
- 1 teaspoon (5g) chia seeds (for garnish)

NUTRITION

- **Kcal per serve**: 330 kcal
- **Carbohydrates**: 37g
- **Sugars**: 3g
- **Fiber**: 10g
- **Protein**: 9g
- **Total Fats**: 18g
- **Saturated Fats**: 3g
- **Monounsaturated Fats**: 10g
- **Polyunsaturated Fats**: 4g
- **Sodium**: 200mg

Scrambled Eggs with Spinach and Feta

1. **Prep Ingredients (2 minutes)** Gather all ingredients. Chop the spinach roughly to ensure it blends well with the eggs, enhancing the meal's texture and nutritional value. Crumble the feta cheese. This step is crucial for a smooth cooking process, ensuring everything is ready for quick assembly.
2. **Beat the Eggs (1 minute)** Crack the eggs into a bowl, season with salt and pepper, and beat well. This process aerates the eggs, making the scrambled eggs fluffy and light, providing a perfect texture that complements the other ingredients' richness and depth of flavor.
3. **Cook Spinach (2 minutes)** Heat olive oil in a non-stick skillet over medium heat. Add the spinach and sauté until wilted. Cooking the spinach before adding eggs ensures it releases most of its moisture, preventing the scrambled eggs from becoming watery.
4. **Add Eggs and Feta (4 minutes)** Pour the beaten eggs over the spinach. Let them set for a moment, then gently stir to create soft curds. Halfway through, sprinkle the crumbled feta over the eggs. The feta adds a creamy, tangy contrast to the mild eggs and spinach.
5. **Serve Immediately (1 minute)** Once the eggs are softly set and still slightly runny, remove from heat. Serve the scrambled eggs immediately to enjoy their creamy texture and the flavors of spinach and feta at their best. Quick serving ensures the eggs don't overcook from residual heat.

INGREDIENTS

- 4 large eggs (about 200g)
- 1 cup (30g) fresh spinach, roughly chopped
- 1/4 cup (60g) feta cheese, crumbled
- 1 tablespoon (15g) olive oil
- Salt to taste (less than 1g)
- Black pepper to taste (less than 1g)

NUTRITION

- **Kcal per serve:** 250 kcal
- **Carbohydrates:** 2g
- **Sugars:** 1g
- **Fiber:** 0.5g
- **Protein:** 14g
- **Total Fats:** 20g
- **Saturated Fats:** 6g
- **Monounsaturated Fats:** 9g
- **Polyunsaturated Fats:** 2g
- **Sodium:** 400mg

Almond Butter and Banana Smoothie

1. **Prepare Ingredients (1 minute)** Peel the banana and break it into chunks. Measure the almond butter, almond milk, and vanilla extract. Preparing ingredients before blending ensures a smooth process, making it easier to combine them efficiently for a creamy smoothie.
2. **Combine Ingredients (2 minutes)** Place the banana chunks, almond butter, almond milk, and vanilla extract into a blender. If you prefer a colder smoothie, add a few ice cubes at this stage. This step is crucial for achieving the perfect texture and flavor of the smoothie.
3. **Blend Until Smooth (2 minutes)** Blend the mixture on high speed until smooth and creamy. It's important to blend thoroughly to ensure the almond butter is fully integrated, creating a uniform and silky smooth texture that's both appealing and easy to drink.
4. **Check Consistency (1 minute)** Pause to check the smoothie's consistency. If it's too thick, add a little more almond milk and blend again. This step allows you to adjust the smoothie to your preferred thickness, ensuring it meets your taste and dietary needs.
5. **Serve Immediately (1 minute)** Pour the smoothie into a tall glass and garnish with a sprinkle of ground almonds and a banana slice. Serving the smoothie immediately ensures maximum freshness and preserves the nutrients, making it a delicious and healthful option for managing Type 2 diabetes.

INGREDIENTS

- 1 large banana (about 120g)
- 2 tablespoons almond butter (about 32g)
- 1 cup unsweetened almond milk (240ml)
- 1/2 teaspoon vanilla extract (2.5ml)
- Ice cubes (optional, for serving)

NUTRITION

- **Kcal per serve**: 210 kcal
- **Carbohydrates**: 24g
- **Sugars**: 12g
- **Fiber**: 4g
- **Protein**: 6g
- **Total Fats**: 12g
- **Saturated Fats**: 1g
- **Monounsaturated Fats**: 7g
- **Polyunsaturated Fats**: 3g
- **Sodium**: 190mg

Cottage Cheese with Pineapple Chunks

1. **Measure Ingredients (1 minute)** Measure out the cottage cheese and fresh pineapple chunks. Choosing fresh pineapple over canned can significantly reduce the sugar content, making it a better choice for managing blood sugar levels in Type 2 diabetes.
2. **Prepare Pineapple (2 minutes)** If using a whole pineapple, peel, core, and cut it into chunks. Fresh pineapple not only adds a burst of flavor but also provides enzymes that aid digestion, making this meal both nutritious and easy to digest.
3. **Assemble in Bowl (2 minutes)** Place the cottage cheese in a serving bowl. Top with the pineapple chunks, distributing them evenly. The creamy texture of the cottage cheese pairs well with the juicy sweetness of the pineapple, offering a delightful contrast.
4. **Optional Garnishes (1 minute)** For added flavor and visual appeal, consider sprinkling a pinch of cinnamon or chia seeds over the top. These optional garnishes can enhance the dish's nutritional profile and add a subtle complexity to the flavors.
5. **Serve Immediately (1 minute)** Enjoy the cottage cheese with pineapple chunks immediately to ensure the freshest taste and texture. This simple, healthful dish is perfect for a quick breakfast or a refreshing snack, offering a balanced combination of protein, carbohydrates, and natural sugars.

INGREDIENTS

- 1 cup (226g) cottage cheese
- 1/2 cup (75g) pineapple chunks, fresh

NUTRITION

- **Kcal per serve:** 180 kcal
- **Carbohydrates:** 15g
- **Sugars:** 12g
- **Fiber:** 1g
- **Protein:** 14g
- **Total Fats:** 5g
- **Saturated Fats:** 3g
- **Monounsaturated Fats:** 1g
- **Polyunsaturated Fats:** 0g
- **Sodium:** 400mg

Quick Oats with Almond Milk and Chia Seeds

1. **Combine Oats and Milk (2 minutes)** In a medium saucepan, combine the quick oats and unsweetened almond milk. Using almond milk enriches the oats with a creamy texture and nutty flavor without additional sugar, making it a hearty base for this diabetic-friendly meal.
2. **Cook Oats (3 minutes)** Bring the oat and almond milk mixture to a boil, then simmer. Stirring prevents the oats from sticking and ensures they cook evenly into a satisfyingly thick consistency, perfect for a filling breakfast or snack.
3. **Flavor Enhancement (1 minute)** Incorporate the cinnamon and optional vanilla extract into the oats. Cinnamon is known for its potential to help manage blood sugar levels, adding not just flavor but also a health benefit, making it an excellent alternative to sweeteners.
4. **Serve (2 minutes)** Evenly distribute the cooked oats into two bowls. This step ensures the warmth and creamy consistency of the oats are maintained, ready for the addition of nutritious toppings.
5. **Add Chia Seeds (2 minutes)** Top each bowl with chia seeds for a nutrient boost. Chia seeds are rich in omega-3 fatty acids, fiber, and protein, which are beneficial for heart health and may aid in blood sugar regulation, making them an ideal topping for those managing Type 2 diabetes.

INGREDIENTS

- 1 cup (90g) quick oats
- 2 cups (480ml) unsweetened almond milk
- 2 tablespoons (30g) chia seeds
- 1/2 teaspoon (2.5ml) cinnamon
- 1/2 teaspoon (2.5ml) vanilla extract (optional, for flavor)

NUTRITION

- **Kcal per serve:** 325 kcal
- **Carbohydrates:** 38g
- **Sugars:** 1g
- **Fiber:** 11g
- **Protein:** 13g
- **Total Fats:** 12g
- **Saturated Fats:** 1g
- **Monounsaturated Fats:** 2g
- **Polyunsaturated Fats:** 9g
- **Sodium:** 180mg

Smoked Salmon and Cream Cheese Cucumber Bites

1. **Prepare the Ingredients (2 minutes)** Wash the cucumber and cut it into thick slices. The cucumber serves as a crisp, refreshing base for the bites, offering a contrast in texture to the creamy cheese and tender salmon.
2. **Mix Cream Cheese (2 minutes)** In a small bowl, mix the softened cream cheese with lemon juice and chopped dill. This mixture will add a tangy, herby flavor to the bites, complementing the smoky taste of the salmon.
3. **Assemble the Bites (3 minutes)** Spread a generous amount of the cream cheese mixture onto each cucumber slice. The cream cheese acts as a glue, holding the salmon in place and adding creaminess to each bite.
4. **Add Smoked Salmon (2 minutes)** Top each cream cheese-covered cucumber slice with a small piece of smoked salmon. The salmon introduces a rich, smoky flavor that pairs beautifully with the creamy and crisp elements of the dish.
5. **Garnish and Serve (1 minute)** Finish each bite with a sprinkle of black pepper and a small sprig of dill. The black pepper adds a slight heat, while the dill provides a fresh, aromatic lift, making these bites ready to impress.

INGREDIENTS

- 1 large cucumber (approximately 8 oz or 225g)
- 4 oz (113g) smoked salmon
- 4 oz (113g) cream cheese, softened
- 1 tablespoon (15g) fresh dill, chopped
- 1 teaspoon (5ml) lemon juice
- Black pepper to taste (less than 1g)

NUTRITION

- **Kcal per serve:** 200 kcal
- **Carbohydrates:** 4g
- **Sugars:** 3g
- **Fiber:** 1g
- **Protein:** 12g
- **Total Fats:** 15g
- **Saturated Fats:** 8g
- **Monounsaturated Fats:** 5g
- **Polyunsaturated Fats:** 2g
- **Sodium:** 670mg

Berry and Nut Yogurt Parfait

1. **Prep Ingredients (2 minutes)** Wash and prepare the mixed fresh berries. Chopping the nuts into smaller pieces enhances the texture and ensures a pleasant crunch in each bite. Preparing your ingredients beforehand streamlines the layering process, making assembly quick and easy.
2. **Mix Yogurt (2 minutes)** Combine the Greek yogurt with vanilla extract. This step infuses the yogurt with a subtle flavor, complementing the natural sweetness of the berries and the nutty crunch. Greek yogurt is chosen for its high protein and low sugar content, ideal for blood sugar management.
3. **Layer the Parfait (3 minutes)** Begin layering the parfait by spooning a layer of Greek yogurt into the bottom of a clear glass. Add a layer of mixed berries, then a sprinkle of chopped nuts. The visual appeal of the layers makes the parfait not only delicious but also a feast for the eyes.
4. **Repeat Layers (2 minutes)** Continue layering yogurt, berries, and nuts until the glass is filled. This method ensures a balanced distribution of flavors and textures, making every spoonful a delightful combination of creamy, crunchy, and juicy.
5. **Garnish and Serve (1 minute)** Top the parfait with a final layer of berries and a sprinkle of chia seeds for added fiber. Serving the parfait immediately ensures the nuts remain crunchy and the berries fresh, offering a nutritious, satisfying treat.

INGREDIENTS

- 1 cup (240g) unsweetened Greek yogurt
- 1/2 cup (70g) mixed fresh berries (strawberries, blueberries, raspberries)
- 2 tablespoons (30g) mixed nuts (almonds, walnuts), chopped
- 1 teaspoon (5ml) vanilla extract (optional, for flavor)
- 1 tablespoon (15ml) chia seeds (optional, for added fiber and nutrients)

NUTRITION

- **Kcal per serve:** 220 kcal
- **Carbohydrates:** 18g
- **Sugars:** 8g
- **Fiber:** 4g
- **Protein:** 20g
- **Total Fats:** 10g
- **Saturated Fats:** 1g
- **Monounsaturated Fats:** 3g
- **Polyunsaturated Fats:** 4g
- **Sodium:** 60mg

Apple Slices with Peanut Butter

1. **Washing and Slicing the Apple (2 minutes)** (Start by thoroughly washing the apple. Once clean, core the apple and cut it into thin slices. This method helps in easy spreading of peanut butter and makes it a handy, quick snack. Thin slices ensure even distribution of flavors and textures.)
2. **Preparing the Peanut Butter (1 minute)** (Take the natural peanut butter and stir it well if oil separation has occurred. This step is crucial to ensure the consistency of the peanut butter is smooth for easy spreading. Natural peanut butter is chosen for its health benefits and minimal processing.)
3. **Spreading the Peanut Butter (3 minutes)** (Spread the natural peanut butter evenly over half of the apple slices. Aim for a thin layer to keep the snack light and healthy. This step combines the crisp freshness of the apple with the creamy richness of the peanut butter.)
4. **Adding Cinnamon (1 minute)** (Lightly sprinkle cinnamon over the peanut butter-coated apple slices. Cinnamon not only adds flavor but also has health benefits, including blood sugar regulation, which is crucial for individuals with type 2 diabetes.)
5. **Serving (3 minutes)** (Arrange the apple slices on a plate, alternating between peanut butter topped and plain slices for a visually appealing presentation. This not only makes the dish inviting but also allows for an even mix of flavors with each bite.)

INGREDIENTS

- 1 large apple (about 8 oz or 225g), cored and sliced
- 2 tablespoons (about 32g) natural peanut butter, unsweetened and unsalted
- A pinch of cinnamon

NUTRITION

- **Kcal:** 150
- **Carbohydrates:** 20g
- **Sugars:** 12g
- **Fiber:** 4g
- **Protein:** 4g
- **Total Fats:** 8g
- **Saturated Fats:** 1.5g
- **Monounsaturated Fats:** 3.5g
- **Polyunsaturated Fats:** 2.5g
- **Sodium:** Less than 5mg

Carrot and Cucumber Sticks with Hummus

1. **Prepare the Vegetables (2 minutes)** - (Peel the carrots and wash the cucumber. Cut both into sticks of roughly equal size, ensuring they are easy to dip. This step is crucial for maintaining a uniform look and making the snack easy to eat.)
2. **Arrange the Platter (2 minutes)** - (Neatly arrange the carrot and cucumber sticks on a serving platter. The key here is to create an appealing display that invites eating. Consider alternating between carrot and cucumber sticks for a visually pleasing pattern.)
3. **Prepare the Hummus (1 minute)** - (Scoop the hummus into a small bowl. If desired, sprinkle a pinch of paprika over the hummus for a touch of color and a slight flavor boost. This adds a Mediterranean flair to the dish.)
4. **Garnish (1 minute)** - (Use parsley sprigs to garnish the platter. This not only adds a fresh flavor but also enhances the visual appeal of the dish. The green of the parsley complements the colors of the carrots and cucumbers.)
5. **Serve (4 minutes)** - (Place the bowl of hummus on the platter with the arranged vegetable sticks. Encourage diners to dip the sticks into the hummus. This final step is about presenting your dish in a way that is inviting to your guests.)

INGREDIENTS

- **2 medium carrots (about 150g each)** - 300g total. Peel and cut into sticks.
- **1 large cucumber (approximately 300g)** - Cut into sticks.
- **1/2 cup (120g) hummus** - Choose a low-fat variety for better health benefits.
- **A pinch of paprika** - To garnish the hummus (optional).
- **A few sprigs of parsley** - For garnish (optional).

NUTRITION

- **Kcal:** Approximately 150 kcal
- **Carbohydrates:** 18g
- **Sugars:** 5g
- **Fiber:** 6g
- **Protein:** 6g
- **Total Fats:** 8g
- **Saturated Fats:** 1g
- **Monounsaturated Fats:** 3g
- **Polyunsaturated Fats:** 4g
- **Sodium:** 300mg

Mixed Nuts and Dried Fruit Trail Mix

1. **Gather Ingredients (2 minutes)** - (Start by assembling all your ingredients. Having everything in front of you simplifies the process and ensures you don't forget anything. This mix is designed to balance sweet and savory while being mindful of a diabetic diet.)
2. **Mix Nuts (2 minutes)** - (Combine almonds, walnuts, and pecans in a large bowl. These nuts are chosen for their low glycemic index, making them ideal for managing blood sugar levels in people with type 2 diabetes.)
3. **Add Seeds and Dried Fruit (2 minutes)** - (Stir in the pumpkin seeds, dried cranberries, and apricots. Pumpkin seeds add crunch and nutrients, while cranberries and apricots offer a hint of sweetness and fiber, enhancing the trail mix's nutritional value.)
4. **Toss Well (2 minutes)** - (Toss the mixture well to ensure an even distribution of flavors and textures. This step is key to creating a harmonious blend where each handful offers a balanced taste of nuts, seeds, and dried fruit.)
5. **Serve or Store (2 minutes)** - (Serve immediately for a fresh snack or store in an airtight container for future snacking. This trail mix is a healthy, portable option for managing hunger and blood sugar levels on the go.)

INGREDIENTS

- **1/4 cup (30g) almonds** - Raw, unsalted.
- **1/4 cup (30g) walnuts** - Raw, unsalted.
- **1/4 cup (30g) pecans** - Raw, unsalted.
- **2 tablespoons (20g) pumpkin seeds** - Raw, unsalted.
- **1/4 cup (40g) dried cranberries** - Unsweetened or sweetened with apple juice.
- **2 tablespoons (30g) dried apricots** - Chopped into small pieces.

NUTRITION

- **Kcal:** Approximately 200 kcal
- **Carbohydrates:** 18g
- **Sugars:** 8g
- **Fiber:** 4g
- **Protein:** 5g
- **Total Fats:** 14g
- **Saturated Fats:** 1.5g
- **Monounsaturated Fats:** 8g
- **Polyunsaturated Fats:** 4.5g
- **Sodium:** 10mg

Ricotta and Berry Whole Wheat Crackers

1. **Prepare the Ingredients (2 minutes)** - (Gather all ingredients. Wash the berries under cold water and pat them dry. This step ensures that the berries are clean and ready to use, enhancing the freshness and safety of your dish.)
2. **Spread Ricotta (2 minutes)** - (Spread an even layer of ricotta cheese on each whole wheat cracker. The ricotta should be smooth and creamy, providing a rich base for the berries to sit on. This step adds protein and calcium to your snack.)
3. **Add Berries (2 minutes)** - (Top each cracker with an assortment of fresh blueberries and raspberries. Arrange them neatly to make the crackers visually appealing. The berries add natural sweetness, vitamins, and antioxidants, making this a nutritious option for managing blood sugar.)
4. **Drizzle Honey (2 minutes)** - (Drizzle a small amount of honey over the berries, if using. This adds a touch of sweetness to the snack without overloading it with sugar. Remember, the honey is optional and should be used sparingly.)
5. **Garnish and Serve (2 minutes)** - (Sprinkle a pinch of cinnamon over the crackers for an extra flavor boost. This not only adds aroma and taste but also has potential blood sugar-lowering effects. Serve immediately to enjoy the freshness of the berries and the creamy ricotta.)

INGREDIENTS

- **4 whole wheat crackers** (about 28g) - Choose a low-sodium, whole grain variety.
- **1/2 cup (120g) ricotta cheese** - Part-skim, for a lower fat content.
- **1/4 cup (35g) fresh blueberries**
- **1/4 cup (35g) fresh raspberries**
- **1 teaspoon (5g) honey** - Optional, for drizzling.
- **A pinch of cinnamon** - Optional, for garnish

NUTRITION

- **Kcal:** Approximately 200 kcal
- **Carbohydrates:** 20g
- **Sugars:** 6g
- **Fiber:** 4g
- **Protein:** 10g
- **Total Fats:** 8g
- **Saturated Fats:** 4g
- **Monounsaturated Fats:** 2g
- **Polyunsaturated Fats:** 1g
- **Sodium:** 150mg

Turkey and Cheese Roll-Ups

1. **Prepare Ingredients (2 minutes)** (Wash and dry the lettuce leaves and tomato. Slice the tomato and avocado thinly. Lay out the turkey slices on a clean surface. Preparing your ingredients beforehand streamlines the assembly process, ensuring freshness and efficiency in your meal preparation.)
2. **Spread Condiments (2 minutes)** (Mix the mayonnaise and mustard in a small bowl. Spread this mixture lightly onto the turkey slices. The combination of these condiments adds a tangy, creamy flavor to the roll-ups without overpowering the natural tastes of the other ingredients.)
3. **Layer and Roll (3 minutes)** (On each turkey slice, place a slice of cheese, followed by slices of tomato and avocado, and a lettuce leaf. Roll them up tightly. The layering creates a balanced distribution of flavors and textures, enhancing the overall taste experience.)
4. **Season (1 minute)** (Once rolled, sprinkle the outside of each roll-up with black pepper to taste. This final seasoning step elevates the flavor profile, adding a slight kick that complements the creamy and savory elements of the roll-up.)
5. **Serve (2 minutes)** Cut each roll-up in half, if desired, and arrange them beautifully on a plate. Serving the dish promptly ensures that the lettuce stays crisp and the flavors remain vibrant, offering a visually appealing and delicious meal.)

INGREDIENTS

- **4 oz (115 g) thinly sliced turkey breast** - Choose low-sodium, high-quality turkey.
- **2 oz (60 g) low-fat cheese slices** - Opt for a type suitable for diabetics, like cheddar or mozzarella.
- **1 medium avocado (about 200 g)** - Provides healthy fats.
- **1 large tomato (about 220 g)** - For freshness and vitamins.
- **4 large lettuce leaves (about 60 g)** - Choose a crisp variety like romaine for wrapping.
- **1 tbsp (15 ml) mustard** - Adds flavor without adding sugar.
- **1 tbsp (15 ml) mayonnaise** - Use a low-fat, sugar-free version.
- **Black pepper to taste**

NUTRITION

- **Kcal:** Approximately 300 kcal
- **Carbohydrates:** 15 g
- **Sugars:** 3 g
- **Fiber:** 7 g
- **Protein:** 25 g
- **Total Fats:** 20 g
- **Saturated Fats:** 5 g
- **Monounsaturated Fats:** 8 g
- **Polyunsaturated Fats:** 3 g
- **Sodium:** 600 mg

Cherry Tomatoes with Mozzarella Balls and Basil (Caprese Skewers)

1. **Wash Ingredients (1 minute)** (Rinse the cherry tomatoes and basil leaves under cold water. Pat dry with a clean towel. This step ensures that the ingredients are clean and safe to eat, while maintaining their freshness and vibrant colors for the skewers.)
2. **Prepare Skewers (4 minutes)** (Thread a cherry tomato, a basil leaf folded in half, and a mozzarella ball onto each skewer. Repeat this process, adding another layer of each ingredient. The alternating colors and textures create an appealing visual and a balanced taste with each bite.)
3. **Drizzle Dressing (2 minutes)** (Whisk together the olive oil and balsamic glaze in a small bowl. Drizzle this dressing over the prepared skewers evenly. The dressing adds a rich, tangy flavor that complements the fresh, creamy, and herbal notes of the other ingredients perfectly.)
4. **Season (1 minute)** (Season the skewers lightly with salt and black pepper. This enhances the flavors of the tomatoes, mozzarella, and basil, bringing out their best qualities without overwhelming the palate or compromising dietary considerations.)
5. **Serve (2 minutes)** (Arrange the skewers on a plate in a visually appealing manner. The quick preparation ensures that the dish is served fresh, allowing the flavors to shine through. This dish is not only a treat for the taste buds but also a feast for the eyes.)

INGREDIENTS

- **12 cherry tomatoes (about 150 g)** - Rich in vitamins and antioxidants.
- **12 small mozzarella balls (about 150 g)** - Use part-skim for lower fat content.
- **24 fresh basil leaves (about 30 g)** - For a burst of flavor and freshness.
- **2 tbsp (30 ml) balsamic glaze** - Choose a low-sugar version suitable for diabetics.
- **1 tbsp (15 ml) olive oil** - Extra virgin for the best flavor and health benefits.
- **Salt to taste (minimal)** - Keep sodium intake in mind for a heart-healthy diet.
- **Black pepper to taste** - Adds depth to the skewers.

NUTRITION

- **Kcal:** Approximately 250 kcal
- **Carbohydrates:** 8 g
- **Sugars:** 4 g
- **Fiber:** 2 g
- **Protein:** 15 g
- **Total Fats:** 18 g
- **Saturated Fats:** 6 g
- **Monounsaturated Fats:** 7 g
- **Polyunsaturated Fats:** 1 g
- **Sodium:** 200 mg

Tuna Salad on Mixed Greens

1. **Mix the Greens (2 minutes)** (Begin by placing the mixed greens into a large bowl. This base will add freshness and volume to your salad, ensuring a satisfying yet light meal. The variety in greens offers a blend of flavors and textures, making every bite interesting.)
2. **Add Tuna and Veggies (3 minutes)** (Drain the canned tuna and flake it onto the greens. Then, distribute the diced tomato and cucumber slices evenly over the salad. This step introduces protein and additional vitamins, creating a balanced nutritional profile suitable for managing type 2 diabetes.)
3. **Prepare the Dressing (2 minutes)** (In a small bowl, whisk together the olive oil, lemon juice, dried oregano, salt, and pepper. This dressing will add a Mediterranean flair to the salad, enhancing the flavors while keeping the meal diabetes-friendly by avoiding added sugars and unhealthy fats.)
4. **Toss the Salad (2 minutes)** (Pour the dressing over the salad and gently toss to coat all the ingredients evenly. This ensures every bite is flavorful. The olive oil provides healthy fats, crucial for heart health, especially important for those with type 2 diabetes.)
5. **Serve (1 minute)** (Divide the salad onto two plates, ensuring an even distribution of greens, tuna, and vegetables. This final step presents the dish in an appetizing way, inviting you to enjoy a healthy, balanced meal that supports diabetes management.)

INGREDIENTS

- 4 oz (about 115g) canned tuna in water, drained
- 2 cups (about 95g) mixed greens (lettuce, spinach, arugula)
- 1 medium tomato (about 150g), diced
- 1/4 cucumber (about 50g), thinly sliced
- 1 tablespoon (about 15ml) olive oil
- 1 tablespoon (about 15ml) lemon juice
- 1/2 teaspoon (about 2.5g) dried oregano
- Salt and pepper to taste (minimal salt for dietary considerations)

NUTRITION

- Kcal: 200
- Carbohydrates: 6g
- Sugars: 3g
- Fiber: 2g
- Protein: 25g
- Total Fats: 10g
- Saturated Fats: 2g
- Monounsaturated Fats: 5g
- Polyunsaturated Fats: 3g
- Sodium: 200mg

Chicken Caesar Salad Wrap

1. **Prepare the Ingredients (2 minutes)** (Start by slicing the grilled chicken breast and chopping the romaine lettuce. Halve the cherry tomatoes. This preparation step ensures all components are ready for assembly, making the wrap construction seamless and efficient.)
2. **Season the Chicken (1 minute)** (Season the sliced chicken with black pepper and garlic powder. This adds flavor depth to the chicken, ensuring the wrap is tasty from the inside out. Seasoning is key for enhancing the natural flavors without adding unnecessary sodium or sugars.)
3. **Assemble the Wraps (3 minutes)** (Lay out the whole wheat wraps on a clean surface. Distribute the romaine lettuce, cherry tomatoes, and seasoned chicken evenly between them. This step is crucial for ensuring a balanced distribution of ingredients, making every bite full of flavor and texture.)
4. **Add Dressing and Cheese (2 minutes)** (Drizzle the low-fat Caesar dressing over the fillings in each wrap and sprinkle with grated Parmesan cheese. The dressing and cheese add a creamy texture and rich flavor, complementing the crunchy lettuce and tomatoes perfectly.)
5. **Roll and Serve (2 minutes)** (Carefully roll each wrap tightly to enclose the fillings. This final step is about securing all the ingredients inside the wrap, making it easy to eat. The wrap should be compact, ensuring a mess-free meal experience.)

INGREDIENTS

- 6 oz (about 170g) grilled chicken breast, sliced
- 2 large whole wheat wraps (about 60g each)
- 1 cup (about 50g) romaine lettuce, chopped
- 1/4 cup (about 30g) cherry tomatoes, halved
- 2 tablespoons (about 30g) low-fat Caesar dressing
- 2 tablespoons (about 30g) grated Parmesan cheese
- 1 teaspoon (about 5g) black pepper
- 1/2 teaspoon (about 2.5g) garlic powder

NUTRITION

- Kcal: 350
- Carbohydrates: 35g
- Sugars: 4g
- Fiber: 5g
- Protein: 38g
- Total Fats: 9g
- Saturated Fats: 3g
- Monounsaturated Fats: 3g
- Polyunsaturated Fats: 2g
- Sodium: 600mg

Smoked Salmon and Avocado Salad

1. **Prepare the Ingredients (2 minutes)** (Start by thinly slicing the smoked salmon and dicing the avocado. Thinly slice the red onion and prepare the mixed salad greens. This step is crucial for ensuring all ingredients are ready for a quick assembly of the salad.)
2. **Mix the Dressing (1 minute)** (In a small bowl, whisk together the extra virgin olive oil and lemon juice. Season with a pinch of salt and pepper. This dressing will add a zesty flavor to the salad, complementing the smoked salmon and avocado beautifully.)
3. **Toss the Salad (3 minutes)** (In a large bowl, combine the mixed salad greens, red onion, and capers. Drizzle the dressing over the salad and toss gently to coat. This ensures every leaf is lightly dressed, enhancing the salad's overall flavor.)
4. **Add Salmon and Avocado (3 minutes)** (Gently fold in the smoked salmon and diced avocado with the dressed salad. This step is key to maintaining the integrity of the delicate salmon and avocado, ensuring they remain intact and visually appealing.)
5. **Serve (1 minute)** (Divide the salad onto two plates, ensuring an even distribution of all ingredients. This final touch is about presenting the salad in an appealing way, making it inviting to eat while maintaining a balanced nutritional profile suitable for type 2 diabetes management.)

INGREDIENTS

- 4 oz (about 115g) smoked salmon, thinly sliced
- 1 medium avocado (about 150g), diced
- 2 cups (about 50g) mixed salad greens
- 1/4 cup (about 30g) red onion, thinly sliced
- 2 tablespoons (about 30g) capers
- 2 tablespoons (about 30ml) extra virgin olive oil
- 1 tablespoon (about 15ml) lemon juice
- Salt and pepper to taste (minimal salt for dietary considerations)

NUTRITION

- Kcal: 300
- Carbohydrates: 9g
- Sugars: 2g
- Fiber: 7g
- Protein: 18g
- Total Fats: 22g
- Saturated Fats: 3g
- Monounsaturated Fats: 14g
- Polyunsaturated Fats: 4g
- Sodium: 400mg

Quinoa Salad with Cucumbers and Feta

1. **Prepare Quinoa (2 minutes)** (Start with cooked quinoa. This can be leftover quinoa or freshly made, cooled to room temperature. Using precooked quinoa helps in assembling the salad quickly, making it an efficient choice for a nutritious meal.)
2. **Dice and Chop (2 minutes)** (Dice the cucumber and finely chop the red onion. This adds crunch and flavor to the salad. The cucumber offers freshness, while the red onion provides a slight sharpness, balancing the dish's overall taste profile.)
3. **Mix the Dressing (1 minute)** (In a small bowl, whisk together the extra virgin olive oil and lemon juice. Season with a pinch of salt and pepper. This simple dressing will add zest and moisture to the salad, enhancing the natural flavors of the other ingredients.)
4. **Combine Ingredients (4 minutes)** (In a large bowl, mix the quinoa, diced cucumber, crumbled feta, chopped red onion, and fresh parsley. Gently fold in the dressing to evenly coat the mixture. The combination of these ingredients offers a balanced mix of textures and flavors.)
5. **Serve (1 minute)** (Divide the salad onto two plates. The final presentation is not only visually appealing but also ensures each serving is packed with a balanced mix of ingredients, offering a satisfying and nutritious meal suitable for managing type 2 diabetes.)

INGREDIENTS

- 1 cup (about 185g) cooked quinoa
- 1 medium cucumber (about 150g), diced
- 1/2 cup (about 75g) feta cheese, crumbled
- 1/4 cup (about 30g) red onion, finely chopped
- 2 tablespoons (about 30ml) extra virgin olive oil
- 1 tablespoon (about 15ml) lemon juice
- 1/4 cup (about 15g) fresh parsley, chopped
- Salt and pepper to taste (minimal salt for dietary considerations)

NUTRITION

- Kcal: 320
- Carbohydrates: 33g
- Sugars: 4g
- Fiber: 5g
- Protein: 11g
- Total Fats: 17g
- Saturated Fats: 6g
- Monounsaturated Fats: 8g
- Polyunsaturated Fats: 2g
- Sodium: 400mg

Turkey Breast and Avocado Lettuce Wraps

1. **Prepare the Ingredients (2 minutes)** (Start by slicing the cooked turkey breast and avocado. Then, wash the lettuce leaves and pat them dry. Preparing these ingredients beforehand streamlines the assembly process, ensuring a quick and efficient meal prep.)
2. **Mix the Dressing (1 minute)** (In a small bowl, combine Greek yogurt and lime juice. Season with a pinch of salt and pepper. This creamy yet tangy dressing will enhance the flavors of the turkey and avocado, adding a refreshing zest to the wraps.)
3. **Assemble the Wraps (4 minutes)** (Lay out the lettuce leaves on a clean surface. Place equal amounts of turkey, avocado, cherry tomatoes, and cucumber slices in the center of each leaf. The variety of ingredients ensures a balance of textures and flavors in every bite.)
4. **Drizzle and Season (2 minutes)** (Evenly drizzle the Greek yogurt dressing over the fillings of each lettuce wrap. This step is crucial for binding the flavors together and adding moisture to the wraps, making them even more delicious and satisfying.)
5. **Serve (1 minute)** (Carefully fold the lettuce over the fillings to close the wraps. This final step is about presenting the meal in an appealing and convenient way, ready to be enjoyed immediately. The wraps offer a light yet protein-rich meal, perfect for managing type 2 diabetes.)

INGREDIENTS

- 6 oz (about 170g) cooked turkey breast, sliced
- 1 large avocado (about 200g), sliced
- 6 large lettuce leaves (such as romaine or iceberg)
- 1/4 cup (about 60g) cherry tomatoes, halved
- 1/4 cup (about 30g) cucumber, thinly sliced
- 2 tablespoons (about 30g) Greek yogurt
- 1 tablespoon (about 15ml) lime juice
- Salt and pepper to taste

NUTRITION

- Kcal: 280
- Carbohydrates: 12g
- Sugars: 3g
- Fiber: 7g
- Protein: 30g
- Total Fats: 14g
- Saturated Fats: 2g
- Monounsaturated Fats: 7g
- Polyunsaturated Fats: 3g
- Sodium: 300mg

Greek Salad with Olives and Feta Cheese

1. **Prepare the Vegetables (2 minutes)** (Begin by dicing the tomato, slicing the cucumber, and thinly slicing the red onion. This variety of vegetables not only adds color and texture to the salad but also provides a mix of vitamins and minerals beneficial for health.)
2. **Combine Salad Ingredients (2 minutes)** (In a large bowl, combine the mixed salad greens, diced tomato, sliced cucumber, and sliced red onion. The base of this salad is a vibrant mix of textures and flavors, creating a delightful and nutritious backdrop for the additional ingredients.)
3. **Add Olives and Feta (1 minute)** (Add the Kalamata olives and crumbled feta cheese to the salad. The salty olives and creamy feta cheese introduce a rich depth of Mediterranean flavors, enhancing the overall taste profile of the salad.)
4. **Dress the Salad (3 minutes)** (Whisk together the extra virgin olive oil, red wine vinegar, dried oregano, salt, and pepper. Drizzle this dressing over the salad, ensuring all ingredients are lightly coated. The dressing ties the flavors together, adding a tangy and herby note.)
5. **Serve (2 minutes)** (Toss the salad gently to mix all the ingredients with the dressing. Divide the salad onto two plates, presenting it in an appetizing way that showcases the freshness and vibrant colors. This step is crucial for a visually appealing presentation that matches the delicious taste.)

INGREDIENTS

- 2 cups (about 100g) mixed salad greens
- 1 medium tomato (about 150g), diced
- 1 medium cucumber (about 150g), sliced
- 1/2 red onion (about 75g), thinly sliced
- 1/2 cup (about 75g) Kalamata olives
- 4 oz (about 115g) feta cheese, crumbled
- 2 tablespoons (about 30ml) extra virgin olive oil
- 1 tablespoon (about 15ml) red wine vinegar
- 1 teaspoon (about 5g) dried oregano
- Salt and pepper to taste (minimal salt for dietary considerations)

NUTRITION

- Kcal: 300
- Carbohydrates: 12g
- Sugars: 6g
- Fiber: 3g
- Protein: 8g
- Total Fats: 24g

Caprese Salad with Balsamic Glaze

1. **Slice Tomatoes and Mozzarella (2 minutes)** (Begin by slicing the tomatoes and mozzarella into even slices. This step is crucial for the visual appeal and balance of flavors in the salad. The freshness of the tomatoes contrasts beautifully with the creamy mozzarella.)
2. **Layer Ingredients (3 minutes)** (Arrange the tomato and mozzarella slices on a plate, alternating them and creating a circular pattern. Tuck fresh basil leaves between the slices. This presentation is not only visually appealing but also allows for an even distribution of flavors in each bite.)
3. **Drizzle with Balsamic Glaze (2 minutes)** (Evenly drizzle the balsamic glaze over the arranged tomatoes, mozzarella, and basil. The glaze adds a sweet and tangy flavor that complements the mildness of the cheese and the freshness of the tomatoes and basil.)
4. **Season (2 minutes)** (Season the salad with a pinch of salt and pepper. Then, drizzle extra virgin olive oil over the top. This finishing touch enhances the flavors and adds a rich, smooth texture to the salad, making it even more delicious.)
5. **Serve (1 minute)** (Present the salad immediately, ensuring it's fresh and the flavors are at their peak.

INGREDIENTS

- 2 large tomatoes (about 450g), sliced
- 8 oz (about 225g) fresh mozzarella cheese, sliced
- 1/4 cup (about 15g) fresh basil leaves
- 2 tablespoons (about 30ml) balsamic glaze
- 2 tablespoons (about 30ml) extra virgin olive oil
- Salt and pepper to taste

NUTRITION

- Kcal: 350
- Carbohydrates: 10g
- Sugars: 8g
- Fiber: 2g
- Protein: 22g
- Total Fats: 25g
- Saturated Fats: 10g
- Monounsaturated Fats: 10g
- Polyunsaturated Fats: 3g
- Sodium: 300mg

Egg Salad on Whole Grain Toast

1. **Boil Eggs (3 minutes)** (Place eggs in a saucepan of boiling water. Cook for 8-10 minutes for hard-boiled eggs. This step ensures the eggs are cooked perfectly, providing a solid base for the salad. Cool them under cold water, then peel.)
2. **Prepare the Toast (2 minutes)** (Toast the whole grain bread slices to your preferred level of crispiness. Whole grain bread is chosen for its higher fiber content, beneficial for blood sugar management in type 2 diabetes.)
3. **Mix the Salad (3 minutes)** (Chop the hard-boiled eggs and mix with Greek yogurt, mustard, paprika, salt, and pepper. This combination creates a creamy, flavorful egg salad with a hint of spice from the paprika and tanginess from the mustard.)
4. **Add Toppings (1 minute)** (Spread the egg salad evenly over the toasted whole grain bread. The creamy salad atop the crunchy toast offers a satisfying texture contrast. Garnish with sliced avocado and chopped chives for freshness and a touch of green.)
5. **Serve (1 minute)** (Serve the egg salad on toast immediately, ensuring the toast remains crunchy and the salad is fresh. This dish is a balanced, nutritious option for breakfast or a light meal, offering a good mix of protein, healthy fats, and fiber.)

INGREDIENTS

- 4 large eggs
- 2 slices whole grain bread (about 70g)
- 2 tablespoons Greek yogurt (about 30g)
- 1 tablespoon mustard (about 15g)
- 1/4 teaspoon paprika (about 1.25g)
- Salt and pepper to taste (minimal salt for dietary considerations)
- 1/4 cup chopped fresh chives (about 15g)
- 1/2 avocado (about 100g), sliced

NUTRITION

- Kcal: 350
- Carbohydrates: 27g
- Sugars: 4g
- Fiber: 7g
- Protein: 20g
- Total Fats: 18g
- Saturated Fats: 4g
- Monounsaturated Fats: 8g
- Polyunsaturated Fats: 4g
- Sodium: 400mg

Spinach and Goat Cheese Stuffed Portobello Mushroom

1. **Prep the Ingredients (2 minutes)** (Wash the Portobello mushrooms and remove the stems. Chop the spinach and mince the garlic. Pre-measure the goat cheese, olive oil, salt, and pepper. This preparation sets the foundation for an efficient and organized cooking process.)
2. **Sauté Spinach and Garlic (3 minutes)**(Heat olive oil in a pan over medium heat. Add garlic and sauté until fragrant, about 1 minute. Add spinach and cook until wilted, about 2 minutes. This step infuses the spinach with garlic flavor and reduces its volume for stuffing.)
3. **Stuff the Mushrooms (2 minutes)**(Place the mushrooms stem side up on a baking sheet. Divide the sautéed spinach between the mushrooms, then top each with half of the goat cheese. The cheese will melt, binding the spinach to the mushroom.)
4. **Broil the Mushrooms (3 minutes)**(Broil the stuffed mushrooms in the oven until the cheese is slightly browned and bubbly, about 3 minutes. This step intensifies the flavors and textures, creating a delicious contrast between the creamy goat cheese and the meaty mushroom.)
5. **Serve (0 minutes)**(Immediately serve the hot, stuffed Portobello mushrooms. This final step ensures the dish is enjoyed at its best, with the goat cheese soft and the spinach perfectly wilted.)

INGREDIENTS

- 2 large Portobello mushrooms (approximately 225g each) (450g total)
- 4 oz (115g) goat cheese
- 2 cups (60g) fresh spinach
- 1 tablespoon (15ml) olive oil
- 2 cloves garlic, minced (about 10g)
- 1/4 teaspoon (1.25g) black pepper
- 1/4 teaspoon (1.25g) salt (optional, may adjust to taste or dietary needs)

NUTRITION

- **Kcal:** 350 kcal
- **Carbohydrates:** 12g
- **Sugars:** 4g
- **Fiber:** 4g
- **Protein:** 22g
- **Total Fats:** 25g
- **Saturated Fats:** 10g
- **Monounsaturated Fats:** 10g
- **Polyunsaturated Fats:** 3g
- **Sodium:** 400mg

Shrimp and Avocado Taco Salad

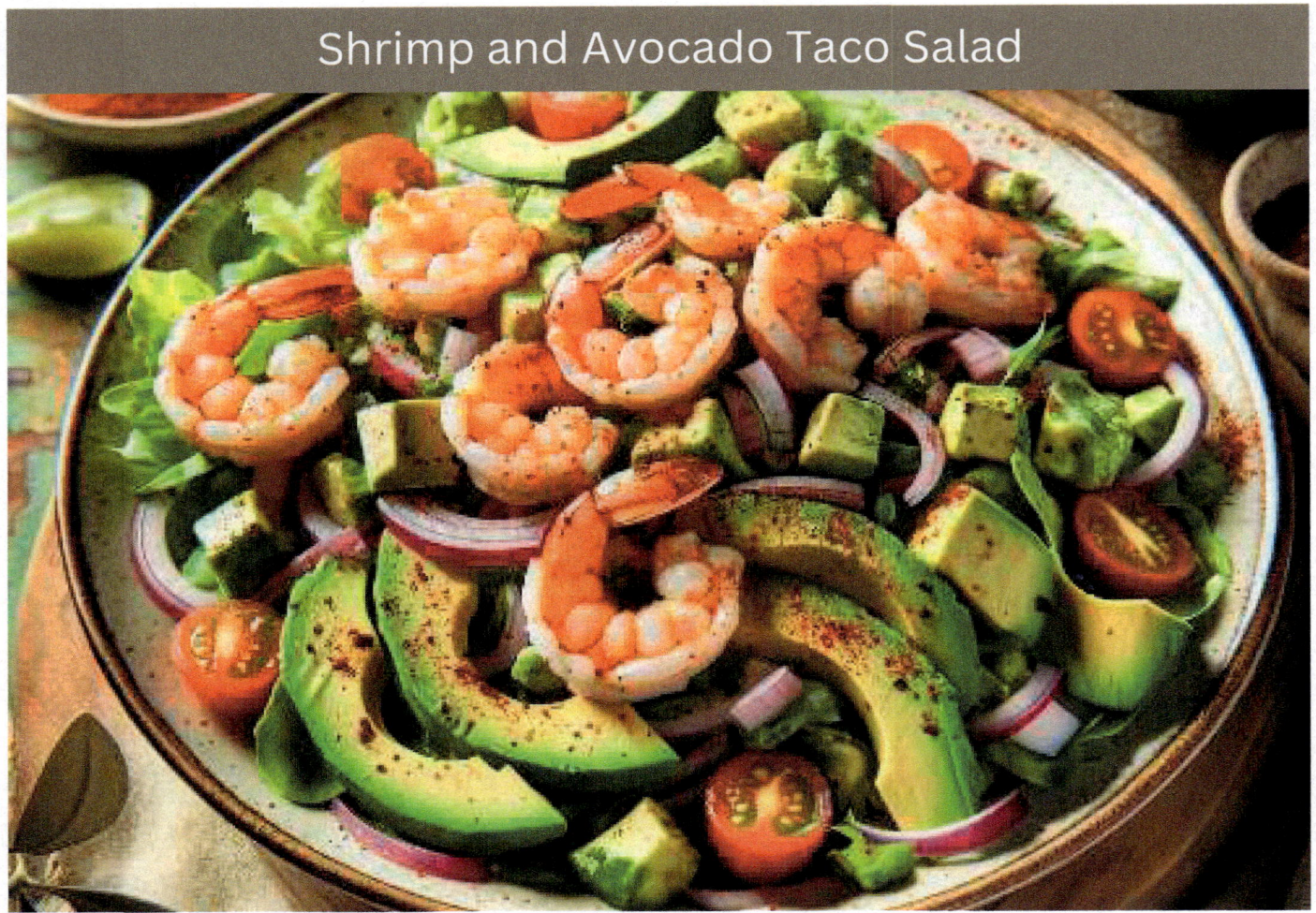

1. **Prep Ingredients (2 minutes)** (Peel and devein shrimp. Dice the avocado, halve cherry tomatoes, and thinly slice red onion. Mix lime juice, olive oil, chili powder, cumin, salt, and pepper in a bowl. This preparation phase sets the foundation for a flavorful salad.)
2. **Cook Shrimp (3 minutes)** (Heat a pan over medium heat. Add shrimp and half of the seasoning mixture. Cook until shrimp are pink and opaque, about 3 minutes, turning halfway. Cooking the shrimp with seasoning enhances their flavor, making them the star of the salad.)
3. **Mix Salad (2 minutes)** (In a large bowl, combine mixed greens, cherry tomatoes, and red onion. Drizzle the remaining lime juice mixture over the salad and toss to coat. The fresh vegetables provide a crunchy base, while the dressing adds zest and ties the flavors together.)
4. **Assemble Salad (2 minutes)** (Add the cooked shrimp and diced avocado to the salad bowl. Gently toss the salad to mix, ensuring even distribution of shrimp and avocado. The avocado adds creaminess, contrasting with the tangy dressing and succulent shrimp.)
5. **Serve (1 minute)** (Divide the salad between two plates, ensuring an even mix of shrimp, avocado, and greens on each. This final step ensures each serving is balanced in flavor and nutrition, offering a visually appealing and satisfying meal.)

INGREDIENTS

- 8 oz (225g) shrimp, peeled and deveined
- 1 large avocado (200g), diced
- 4 cups (120g) mixed salad greens
- 1/2 cup (75g) cherry tomatoes, halved
- 1/4 cup (40g) red onion, thinly sliced
- 2 tablespoons (30ml) lime juice
- 1 tablespoon (15ml) olive oil
- 1/2 teaspoon (2.5g) chili powder
- 1/4 teaspoon (1.25g) ground cumin
- 1/4 teaspoon (1.25g) salt (optional, can adjust to taste or dietary needs)
- 1/4 teaspoon (1.25g) black pepper

NUTRITION

- **Kcal:** 400 kcal
- **Carbohydrates:** 20g
- **Sugars:** 5g
- **Fiber:** 8g
- **Protein:** 30g
- **Total Fats:** 25g
- **Saturated Fats:** 4g
- **Monounsaturated Fats:** 15g
- **Polyunsaturated Fats:** 5g
- **Sodium:** 350mg

Garlic Lemon Shrimp Over Zucchini Noodles

1. **Prepare Ingredients (2 minutes)** (Spiralize the zucchinis into noodles. Peel and devein shrimp. Mince garlic. This preparation step ensures that all components are ready for quick cooking, essential for a meal designed to be both nutritious and suitable for those managing type 2 diabetes.)
2. **Cook Shrimp (3 minutes)** (Heat one tablespoon of olive oil in a pan over medium heat. Add shrimp, season with salt and pepper, and cook until pink and opaque, about 3 minutes. Cooking shrimp properly ensures they are succulent and flavorful, a perfect protein source for this dish.)
3. **Sauté Garlic (1 minute)** (Remove shrimp from the pan. Add the remaining olive oil and minced garlic to the pan, sautéing until fragrant. This step infuses the oil with garlic flavor, creating a aromatic base for the zucchini noodles.)
4. **Cook Zucchini Noodles (3 minutes)** (Add zucchini noodles to the pan with garlic oil. Sauté until just tender, about 3 minutes. Stir in lemon juice and red pepper flakes, heating through. This ensures the noodles are al dente, absorbing the garlic and lemon flavors.)
5. **Combine and Serve (1 minute)** (Return shrimp to the pan with zucchini noodles, tossing to combine. Garnish with fresh parsley. This final step unites all flavors, presenting a dish that is visually appealing, nutritious, and suitable for a diabetic diet.)

INGREDIENTS

- 8 oz (225g) shrimp, peeled and deveined
- 2 medium zucchinis (500g), spiralized into noodles
- 2 tablespoons (30ml) olive oil
- 2 cloves garlic, minced (about 10g)
- Juice of 1 lemon (about 45ml)
- 1/4 teaspoon (1.25g) red pepper flakes
- 1/4 teaspoon (1.25g) salt (optional, can adjust to taste or dietary needs)
- 1/4 teaspoon (1.25g) black pepper
- Fresh parsley, chopped (for garnish,

NUTRITION

- **Kcal:** 320 kcal
- **Carbohydrates:** 12g
- **Sugars:** 4g
- **Fiber:** 3g
- **Protein:** 25g
- **Total Fats:** 20g
- **Saturated Fats:** 3g
- **Monounsaturated Fats:** 12g
- **Polyunsaturated Fats:** 3g
- **Sodium:** 350mg (without added salt)

Quick Beef Stir-Fry with Bell Peppers

1. **Prep Ingredients (2 minutes)** (Thinly slice the beef and bell peppers. Mince the garlic. This preparation step ensures quick and even cooking, critical for a dish designed for both nutritional balance and convenience, especially suitable for those managing type 2 diabetes.)
2. **Heat Oil (1 minute)** (Heat olive oil in a large pan over medium-high heat. This step forms the base for sautéing, allowing for a quick sear of the beef, essential for locking in flavors.)
3. **Cook Beef (2 minutes)** (Add beef to the pan and stir-fry until just browned, about 2 minutes. This ensures the beef is cooked through yet remains tender, a key component of the dish's appeal.)
4. **Add Vegetables and Seasonings (3 minutes)** (Add bell peppers, garlic, soy sauce, sesame oil, ginger, and black pepper to the pan. Stir-fry until vegetables are tender-crisp, about 3 minutes. This combination infuses the dish with a rich blend of flavors while maintaining a nutritious profile.)
5. **Garnish and Serve (2 minutes)** (Remove from heat and garnish with fresh cilantro. This final touch adds a burst of color and fresh flavor, completing the dish with a visually appealing presentation that's ready to serve.)

INGREDIENTS

- 8 oz (225g) lean beef, thinly sliced
- 1 red bell pepper (150g), thinly sliced
- 1 yellow bell pepper (150g), thinly sliced
- 1 tablespoon (15ml) olive oil
- 2 cloves garlic, minced (about 10g)
- 1 tablespoon (15ml) low-sodium soy sauce
- 1 teaspoon (5ml) sesame oil
- 1/2 teaspoon (2.5g) ground ginger
- 1/4 teaspoon (1.25g) black pepper
- Fresh cilantro, chopped (for garnish, optional)

NUTRITION

- **Kcal**: 300 kcal
- **Carbohydrates**: 10g
- **Sugars**: 5g
- **Fiber**: 2g
- **Protein**: 25g
- **Total Fats**: 18g
- **Saturated Fats**: 4g
- **Monounsaturated Fats**: 10g
- **Polyunsaturated Fats**: 3g
- **Sodium**: 400mg

Pan-Seared Salmon with Spinach Salad

1. **Prep Ingredients (2 minutes)** (Rinse the salmon and pat dry. Slice the red onion and mince the garlic. Measure out the lemon juice, olive oil, salt, and pepper. This preparation step ensures all ingredients are ready for a quick and efficient cooking process.)
2. **Cook Salmon (3 minutes)** (Heat half the olive oil in a pan over medium-high heat. Season the salmon with salt and pepper, then place in the pan, skin-side down. Cook until the skin is crisp, about 3 minutes, ensuring a flavorful crust.)
3. **Flip and Finish Salmon (2 minutes)** (Flip the salmon and cook for another 2 minutes, or until desired doneness. The quick sear locks in moisture, ensuring the salmon is tender and flavorful, perfect for a nutritious, diabetes-friendly meal.)
4. **Prepare Salad (2 minutes)** (Toss the spinach, red onion, almonds, and minced garlic in a bowl. Drizzle with the remaining olive oil and lemon juice. This combination creates a fresh, nutrient-rich base for the salmon, aligning with dietary needs for type 2 diabetes.)
5. **Serve (1 minute)** (Plate the salmon on top of the spinach salad. This final step marries the warm, rich flavors of the salmon with the cool, crisp salad, offering a balanced, visually appealing dish suitable for managing diabetes.)

INGREDIENTS

- 2 salmon fillets (6 oz or 170g each)
- 4 cups (120g) fresh spinach
- 1 tablespoon (15ml) olive oil
- 1 teaspoon (5ml) lemon juice
- 1 clove garlic, minced (about 5g)
- 1/4 teaspoon (1.25g) salt (optional, can adjust to taste or dietary needs)
- 1/4 teaspoon (1.25g) black pepper
- 1/4 cup (30g) sliced almonds, toasted
- 1/2 red onion, thinly sliced (about 50g)

NUTRITION

- **Kcal:** 400 kcal
- **Carbohydrates:** 9g
- **Sugars:** 2g
- **Fiber:** 4g
- **Protein:** 35g
- **Total Fats:** 25g
- **Saturated Fats:** 4g
- **Monounsaturated Fats:** 10g
- **Polyunsaturated Fats:** 8g
- **Sodium:** 300mg

Chicken Fajitas with Pre-Cut Veggies

1. **Prep Ingredients (2 minutes)** (Thinly slice the chicken breasts. Ensure pre-cut veggies are ready. Measure out olive oil, fajita seasoning, and lime juice. Prepping ingredients beforehand simplifies cooking, making it swift and efficient, especially beneficial for those managing type 2 diabetes with dietary considerations.)
2. **Marinate Chicken (1 minute)** (Toss chicken slices with half the fajita seasoning and lime juice. Quick marination infuses flavor into the chicken, enhancing the dish's overall taste profile, critical for a satisfying, diabetes-friendly meal.)
3. **Cook Chicken (3 minutes)** (Heat olive oil in a large pan over medium-high heat. Add chicken and cook until no longer pink, about 3 minutes. Cooking chicken thoroughly is key to ensuring a safe, protein-rich component of the fajitas.)
4. **Sauté Veggies (3 minutes)** (Add pre-cut bell peppers and onion to the pan, sprinkling with the remaining fajita seasoning. Sauté until vegetables are tender-crisp, about 3 minutes. This step enriches the dish with flavors and textures, aligning with a nutritious diet plan for type 2 diabetes.)
5. **Assemble and Serve (1 minute)** (Warm tortillas, if using. Serve chicken and veggies with tortillas, garnishing with fresh cilantro. This final step combines all elements, presenting a colorful, appetizing dish that balances taste with nutritional needs.)

INGREDIENTS

- 2 chicken breasts (16 oz or 450g), thinly sliced
- 2 cups (300g) pre-cut mixed bell peppers (red, yellow, green)
- 1 medium onion (150g), pre-cut into slices
- 1 tablespoon (15ml) olive oil
- 1 tablespoon (15g) fajita seasoning
- 1 lime (juice) (about 30ml)
- Fresh cilantro, chopped (for garnish, optional)
- 4 whole wheat tortillas (for serving, optional)

NUTRITION

- **Kcal:** 350 kcal
- **Carbohydrates:** 25g
- **Sugars:** 5g
- **Fiber:** 4g
- **Protein:** 35g
- **Total Fats:** 10g
- **Saturated Fats:** 2g
- **Monounsaturated Fats:** 5g
- **Polyunsaturated Fats:** 2g
- **Sodium:** 500mg

Tofu and Vegetable Stir-Fry with Soy Sauce

1. **Prep Ingredients (2 minutes)** (Press tofu to remove excess water and cube. Prepare vegetables if not already pre-cut. Measure soy sauce, sesame oil, and prepare garlic and ginger. Getting ingredients ready beforehand streamlines the cooking process, essential for a quick, nutritious meal suitable for diabetes management.)
2. **Cook Tofu (3 minutes)** (Heat half the olive oil in a pan over medium-high heat. Add tofu cubes, cooking until golden on all sides, about 3 minutes. Crisping tofu adds texture and flavor, making it a satisfying protein source for this diabetes-friendly dish.)
3. **Sauté Vegetables (3 minutes)** (Remove tofu; add remaining olive oil. Sauté garlic, ginger, and mixed vegetables until crisp-tender, about 3 minutes. Adding aromatics early enhances flavor, while quick cooking retains nutrients essential for a balanced diabetic diet.)
4. **Combine and Season (1 minute)** (Return tofu to pan with vegetables. Add soy sauce, sesame oil, and black pepper, stirring to combine. This step infuses the dish with savory flavors, ensuring a harmonious blend of ingredients.)
5. **Garnish and Serve (1 minute)** (Plate the stir-fry, garnishing with fresh cilantro if desired. This final touch adds a burst of color and freshness, elevating the visual appeal and taste of the meal, ready to be enjoyed.)

INGREDIENTS

- 8 oz (225g) firm tofu, pressed and cubed
- 2 cups (150g) mixed vegetables (broccoli, bell peppers, carrots), pre-cut
- 1 tbsp (15ml) olive oil
- 2 tbsp (30ml) low-sodium soy sauce
- 1 tsp (5ml) sesame oil
- 1 clove garlic, minced (about 5g)
- 1 tsp (5g) fresh ginger, grated
- 1/4 tsp (1.25g) black pepper
- Fresh cilantro, chopped

NUTRITION

- **Kcal:** 250 kcal
- **Carbohydrates:** 15g
- **Sugars:** 5g
- **Fiber:** 4g
- **Protein:** 15g
- **Total Fats:** 15g
- **Saturated Fats:** 2g
- **Monounsaturated Fats:** 8g
- **Polyunsaturated Fats:** 4g
- **Sodium:** 600mg

Spaghetti Squash with Marinara Sauce (Microwave Cooked)

1. **Prep Squash (2 minutes)** (Cut the spaghetti squash in half lengthwise and scoop out the seeds. This preparation is crucial for cooking it evenly in the microwave, making it a quick and easy method suitable for managing type 2 diabetes through a nutritious diet.)
2. **Microwave Squash (5 minutes)** (Place squash halves cut-side down in a microwave-safe dish with a little water. Microwave on high for about 5 minutes, or until tender. Cooking spaghetti squash in the microwave is a time-efficient way to prepare a low-carb, diabetes-friendly pasta alternative.)
3. **Prepare Sauce (1 minute)** (While squash cooks, heat marinara sauce in a microwave-safe bowl for about 1 minute, or until warm. Choosing a low-sodium sauce helps manage sodium intake, important for a diabetic-friendly diet.)
4. **Shred Squash (1 minute)** (Let squash cool slightly, then use a fork to scrape out the flesh into spaghetti-like strands. This step transforms the squash into a delicious, low-carb substitute for traditional pasta, aligning with dietary guidelines for type 2 diabetes.)
5. **Assemble and Serve (1 minute)** (Toss spaghetti squash strands with olive oil, salt, and pepper. Serve topped with warm marinara sauce, garnished with basil and Parmesan if desired. This final touch adds flavor and visual appeal, making the dish both nutritious and satisfying.)

INGREDIENTS

- 1 medium spaghetti squash (about 2 lbs or 900g)
- 1 cup (240ml) low-sodium marinara sauce
- 1 tablespoon (15ml) olive oil
- 1/2 teaspoon (2.5g) salt (optional, can adjust to taste or dietary needs)
- 1/4 teaspoon (1.25g) black pepper
- Fresh basil, chopped (for garnish, optional)
- Grated Parmesan cheese

NUTRITION

- **Kcal:** 200 kcal
- **Carbohydrates:** 30g
- **Sugars:** 12g
- **Fiber:** 7g
- **Protein:** 4g
- **Total Fats:** 7g
- **Saturated Fats:** 1g
- **Monounsaturated Fats:** 5g
- **Polyunsaturated Fats:** 1g
- **Sodium:** 400mg

Grilled Chicken Breast with Steamed Broccoli

1. **Prep Ingredients (2 minutes)** (Season chicken breasts with salt and pepper. Prepare broccoli florets for steaming. This initial preparation ensures that the cooking process will be efficient and straightforward, aligning with dietary needs for managing type 2 diabetes.)
2. **Grill Chicken (4 minutes)** (Grill chicken breasts over medium-high heat, 2 minutes per side, until fully cooked. Grilling provides a delicious char and locks in flavors, making the chicken both appetizing and a lean protein source for a diabetes-friendly diet.)
3. **Steam Broccoli (3 minutes)** (While chicken cooks, steam broccoli in a microwave-safe dish with a bit of water, covered, for about 3 minutes. Steaming preserves nutrients and offers a tender yet crisp texture, complementing the grilled chicken.)
4. **Rest Chicken (1 minute)** (Let grilled chicken rest for a minute after cooking. This ensures juices redistribute, keeping the meat moist and tender. It's a crucial step for achieving the perfect texture and enhancing the overall taste of the dish.)
5. **Serve (0 minutes)** (Slice the chicken and serve alongside the steamed broccoli. Optionally, add a squeeze of lemon for added flavor. This final step combines all elements, presenting a nutritious, balanced meal ideal for managing diabetes.)

INGREDIENTS

- 2 chicken breasts (8 oz or 225g each)
- 2 cups (300g) broccoli florets
- 1 tablespoon (15ml) olive oil
- 1/2 teaspoon (2.5g) salt (optional, can adjust to taste or dietary needs)
- 1/4 teaspoon (1.25g) black pepper
- 1 lemon (for serving, optional)

NUTRITION

- **Kcal**: 300 kcal
- **Carbohydrates**: 10g
- **Sugars**: 3g
- **Fiber**: 4g
- **Protein**: 40g
- **Total Fats**: 10g
- **Saturated Fats**: 2g
- **Monounsaturated Fats**: 6g
- **Polyunsaturated Fats**: 2g
- **Sodium**: 300mg

Pork Tenderloin Medallions with Apple Slaw

1. **Prep Ingredients (2 minutes)** (Slice pork tenderloin into medallions. Shred cabbage and julienne the apple. Measuring and preparing these ingredients beforehand streamlines the cooking process, aligning with the dietary management of type 2 diabetes through quick, nutritious meals.)
2. **Cook Pork (3 minutes)** (Heat olive oil in a skillet over medium-high heat. Season pork medallions with salt and pepper, and cook until golden and cooked through, about 1.5 minutes per side. This ensures a flavorful, protein-rich component to the meal.)
3. **Mix Slaw (2 minutes)** (In a bowl, combine shredded cabbage, julienned apple, apple cider vinegar, Dijon mustard, salt, and pepper. Toss well to coat. The slaw adds a fresh, tangy contrast to the savory pork, enhancing the dish's overall flavor profile.)
4. **Rest Pork (2 minutes)** (Let the cooked pork medallions rest for a couple of minutes. Resting meat is crucial for retaining its juices, ensuring that each bite is tender and delicious, making the meal more enjoyable and satisfying.)
5. **Serve (1 minute)** (Plate the pork medallions alongside the apple slaw. Garnish with fresh parsley for a burst of color and flavor. This final step presents a balanced, visually appealing dish that caters to the nutritional needs of those managing type 2 diabetes.)

INGREDIENTS

- 1 lb (450g) pork tenderloin, sliced into medallions
- 2 cups (200g) shredded cabbage
- 1 medium apple (150g), julienned
- 1 tablespoon (15ml) olive oil
- 2 tbsp (30ml) apple cider vinegar
- 1 teaspoon (5ml) Dijon mustard
- 1/2 teaspoon (2.5g) salt
- 1/4 teaspoon (1.25g) black pepper
- Fresh parsley, chopped (for garnish, optional)

NUTRITION

- **Kcal:** 350 kcal
- **Carbohydrates:** 15g
- **Sugars:** 10g
- **Fiber:** 3g
- **Protein:** 40g
- **Total Fats:** 15g
- **Saturated Fats:** 3g
- **Monounsaturated Fats:** 8g
- **Polyunsaturated Fats:** 3g
- **Sodium:** 400mg

Balsamic Glazed Steak Bites and Tomatoes

1. **Prep Ingredients (2 minutes)** (Cube the steak and halve the cherry tomatoes. Measure the balsamic vinegar, olive oil, and Dijon mustard. This preparation phase is essential for ensuring the cooking process is efficient, especially beneficial for those managing type 2 diabetes through dietary means.)
2. **Cook Steak (3 minutes)** (Heat olive oil in a skillet over medium-high heat. Add steak cubes, seasoning with salt and pepper, and cook until browned on all sides, about 3 minutes. This method ensures the steak is flavorful and juicy, providing a rich protein source.)
3. **Add Tomatoes (2 minutes)** (Add cherry tomatoes to the skillet, cooking until they begin to soften, about 2 minutes. The tomatoes add a fresh, tangy contrast to the savory steak, enhancing the dish's overall flavor profile.)
4. **Glaze (2 minutes)** (Stir in balsamic vinegar and Dijon mustard, cooking for an additional 2 minutes to allow the glaze to thicken and coat the steak and tomatoes. This glaze adds a rich, tangy dimension to the dish, tying all the flavors together.)
5. **Garnish and Serve (1 minute)** (Remove from heat and garnish with fresh basil. This final touch adds a burst of color and freshness, presenting a balanced, visually appealing dish that meets the nutritional needs of those with type 2 diabetes.)

INGREDIENTS

- 1 lb (450g) steak (e.g., sirloin or tenderloin), cut into cubes
- 1 cup (150g) cherry tomatoes
- 2 tablespoons (30ml) balsamic vinegar
- 1 tablespoon (15ml) olive oil
- 1 teaspoon (5g) Dijon mustard
- 1/2 teaspoon (2.5g) salt (optional, can adjust to taste or dietary needs)
- 1/4 teaspoon (1.25g) black pepper
- Fresh basil, chopped

NUTRITION

- **Kcal:** 400 kcal
- **Carbohydrates:** 8g
- **Sugars:** 6g
- **Fiber:** 2g
- **Protein:** 50g
- **Total Fats:** 20g
- **Saturated Fats:** 5g
- **Monounsaturated Fats:** 10g
- **Polyunsaturated Fats:** 3g
- **Sodium:** 350mg

Cauliflower Fried Rice with Egg and Peas

1. **Prep Ingredients (2 minutes)** (Prepare cauliflower rice, either by pulsing in a food processor or using pre-riced cauliflower. Thaw peas, mince garlic, and slice green onions. This preparation step is essential for a quick cooking process, aligning with the dietary management of type 2 diabetes.)
2. **Cook Eggs (2 minutes)** (Heat half the olive oil in a pan. Scramble the eggs until fully cooked, then set aside. Eggs provide a high-quality protein source, crucial for a balanced diabetic meal.)
3. **Sauté Garlic and Peas (2 minutes)** (In the same pan, add the remaining olive oil, garlic, and peas. Sauté for about 2 minutes, until fragrant and peas are heated through. This adds flavor and nutrients to the dish.)
4. **Add Cauliflower Rice (3 minutes)** (Stir in cauliflower rice, seasoning with salt, pepper, and soy sauce. Cook until the cauliflower is tender, about 3 minutes. Cauliflower rice is a low-carb alternative to traditional rice, making it ideal for diabetes management.)
5. **Combine and Serve (1 minute)** (Mix in the scrambled eggs with the cauliflower rice mixture. Garnish with green onions. This final step ensures the dish is well-combined, offering a visually appealing and nutritious meal suitable for those with type 2 diabetes.)

INGREDIENTS

- 4 cups (400g) cauliflower rice
- 2 large eggs
- 1 cup (150g) frozen peas, thawed
- 2 tablespoons (30ml) olive oil
- 2 cloves garlic, minced (about 10g)
- 1/2 teaspoon (2.5g) salt (optional, can adjust to taste or dietary needs)
- 1/4 teaspoon (1.25g) black pepper
- 2 green onions, sliced (for garnish, optional)
- 1 tablespoon (15ml) low-sodium soy sauce

NUTRITION

- **Kcal:** 300 kcal
- **Carbohydrates:** 18g
- **Sugars:** 5g
- **Fiber:** 6g
- **Protein:** 14g
- **Total Fats:** 20g
- **Saturated Fats:** 3g
- **Monounsaturated Fats:** 12g
- **Polyunsaturated Fats:** 3g
- **Sodium:** 500mg

Avocado and Black Bean Salad

1. **Prep Ingredients (2 minutes)** (Start by dicing the avocado and finely chopping the red onion. Halve the cherry tomatoes. This quick preparation step ensures all ingredients are ready for assembly, streamlining the salad-making process for a fast and efficient start.)
2. **Mix the Salad (3 minutes)** (Combine the diced avocado, rinsed black beans, halved cherry tomatoes, and chopped red onion in a large mixing bowl. This step is crucial for blending the flavors and textures that will define the salad's character and appeal.)
3. **Season (2 minutes)** (Season the mixture with ground cumin, salt, and pepper. Drizzle with lime juice and olive oil, then gently toss to coat evenly. Seasoning is key to enhancing the natural flavors, with lime adding a fresh zest and olive oil enriching the salad's texture.)
4. **Add Freshness (2 minutes)** (Sprinkle the chopped fresh cilantro over the salad. This final touch introduces a burst of freshness and color, lifting the overall flavor profile. Cilantro adds a distinct taste that complements the creamy avocado and the earthy black beans.)
5. **Serve (1 minute)** (Transfer the salad to serving dishes. This last step is about presentation, ensuring each plate is generously filled, invitingly arranged, and ready to be enjoyed immediately for the freshest taste.)

INGREDIENTS

- 1 avocado (about 200g), diced
- 1 cup (about 170g) canned black beans, rinsed and drained
- 1/2 cup (about 90g) cherry tomatoes, halved
- 1/4 cup (about 40g) red onion, finely chopped
- 2 tablespoons (about 30ml) lime juice
- 1 tablespoon (about 15ml) olive oil
- 1/4 teaspoon (about 1g) ground cumin
- Salt and pepper to taste
- 2 tablespoons (about 8g) fresh cilantro, chopped

NUTRITION

- Kcal: 350
- Carbohydrates: 37g
- Sugars: 5g
- Fiber: 15g
- Protein: 10g
- Total Fats: 20g
- Saturated Fats: 3g
- Monounsaturated Fats: 10g
- Polyunsaturated Fats: 3g
- Sodium: 200mg

Vegan Tacos with Refried Beans and Avocado

1. **Prep the Veggies (2 minutes)** (Start by dicing the tomatoes and slicing the avocado. Shred the lettuce finely. If using frozen corn, thaw it now. This colorful array of veggies not only adds a visual appeal but also ensures a fiber-rich meal, beneficial for blood sugar management.)
2. **Season the Beans (1 minute)** (Mix the refried beans with ground cumin, chili powder, and garlic powder. Adding these spices not only enhances the flavor without adding extra sodium but also incorporates antioxidants, which are beneficial for overall health, especially for individuals with type 2 diabetes.)
3. **Warm the Tortillas (2 minutes)** (Heat the tortillas in a dry skillet over medium heat for about a minute on each side. Warming them makes them more pliable and brings out their nutty flavor, creating a perfect base for your taco fillings.)
4. **Assemble the Tacos (3 minutes)** (Spread the seasoned refried beans onto the warm tortillas. Top with shredded lettuce, diced tomatoes, corn, and slices of avocado. Drizzle lime juice over each taco for a zesty finish. This assembly is not only quick but ensures a balanced distribution of flavors and nutrients.)
5. **Serve (2 minutes)** (Once assembled, serve the tacos immediately. This final step is about bringing everything together on the plate in a visually appealing way, ensuring each bite is packed with flavor, fiber, and nutrients essential for managing type 2 diabetes.)

INGREDIENTS

- 1 cup (225g) refried beans, low sodium
- 1 avocado, medium-sized (200g)
- 4 whole wheat tortillas (200g)
- 1/2 cup (50g) shredded lettuce
- 1/4 cup (60g) diced tomatoes
- 1/4 cup (60g) corn, fresh or frozen
- 2 tablespoons (30ml) lime juice
- 1/4 teaspoon (1g) ground cumin
- 1/4 teaspoon (1g) chili powder
- 1/4 teaspoon (1g) garlic powder
- Salt to taste (minimal)

NUTRITION

- Kcal: 350
- Carbohydrates: 45g
- Sugars: 5g
- Fiber: 15g
- Protein: 12g
- Total Fats: 15g
- Saturated Fats: 2g
- Monounsaturated Fats: 7g
- Polyunsaturated Fats: 3g
- Sodium: 200mg

Spicy Chickpea Lettuce Wraps

1. **Mix Spices and Chickpeas (2 minutes)** (Combine chickpeas, olive oil, lemon juice, ground cumin, chili powder, garlic powder, and paprika in a bowl. This mixture introduces a blend of flavors and antioxidants, supporting blood sugar control and adding a spicy kick to the wraps.)
2. **Prepare the Veggies (2 minutes)** (Chop the red onion and halve the cherry tomatoes. Preparing fresh vegetables ensures a burst of flavor and a rich supply of vitamins and minerals, contributing to a balanced diet essential for managing diabetes.)
3. **Warm the Chickpeas (2 minutes)** (Heat the seasoned chickpeas in a microwave for about a minute or until warm. Warming enhances the flavors and makes the dish more comforting, especially when contrasted with the cool, crisp lettuce leaves.)
4. **Assemble the Wraps (3 minutes)** (Lay out the lettuce leaves and spoon the chickpea mixture onto each leaf. Top with cherry tomatoes and red onion. The combination of spicy chickpeas with the fresh crunch of lettuce and veggies offers a nutritious and satisfying meal.)
5. **Serve (1 minute)** (Once assembled, serve the wraps immediately. This final touch ensures that every wrap is fresh and full of flavor, making it a perfect, quick, and healthy meal for individuals with type 2 diabetes.)

INGREDIENTS

- 1 can (15 oz or 425g) chickpeas, rinsed and drained
- 8 large lettuce leaves (romaine or butter lettuce) (200g)
- 1/2 cup (75g) cherry tomatoes, halved
- 1/4 cup (40g) red onion, finely chopped
- 2 tablespoons (30ml) lemon juice
- 1 tablespoon (15ml) olive oil
- 1/2 teaspoon (2g) ground cumin
- 1/2 teaspoon (2g) chili powder
- 1/4 teaspoon (1g) garlic powder
- 1/4 teaspoon (1g) paprika
- Salt to taste (minimal)

NUTRITION

- Kcal: 300
- Carbohydrates: 35g
- Sugars: 8g
- Fiber: 12g
- Protein: 10g
- Total Fats: 14g
- Saturated Fats: 2g
- Monounsaturated Fats: 8g
- Polyunsaturated Fats: 3g
- Sodium: 300mg

Quick Veggie and Hummus Sandwich

1. **Prep the Veggies (3 minutes)** (Slice the cucumber, tomatoes, red onion, and bell pepper. These fresh vegetables are low in calories yet rich in fiber and essential nutrients, making them ideal for managing blood sugar levels and adding crunch and color to the sandwich.)
2. **Toast the Bread (2 minutes)** (Lightly toast the whole grain bread slices in a toaster until they are just golden. Using whole grain bread adds fiber and nutrients, which are important for blood sugar control and provide a satisfying texture contrast to the creamy hummus.)
3. **Spread the Hummus (2 minutes)** (Spread the hummus evenly over the toasted bread slices. Hummus is a great source of protein and fiber, making it an excellent choice for people with type 2 diabetes. It adds creaminess and depth of flavor to the sandwich.)
4. **Assemble the Sandwich (2 minutes)** (Layer the sliced veggies and mixed salad greens on two of the hummus-spread slices. Drizzle with olive oil and sprinkle with black pepper and minimal salt. The combination of vegetables provides a variety of textures and flavors, making the sandwich filling and nutritious.)
5. **Serve (1 minute)** (Top with the remaining slices of bread, cut each sandwich in half, and serve immediately. This step presents the sandwich in a more appealing way and makes it easier to eat, ensuring a balance of flavors and nutrients in every bite.)

INGREDIENTS

- 4 slices of whole grain bread (140g)
- 1/2 cup (120g) hummus
- 1 medium cucumber, sliced (200g)
- 2 medium tomatoes, sliced (180g)
- 1/4 red onion, thinly sliced (30g)
- 1/2 bell pepper, thinly sliced (90g)
- 1/2 cup (30g) mixed salad greens
- 1 tablespoon (15ml) olive oil
- 1/2 teaspoon (2g) black pepper
- Salt to taste (minimal)

NUTRITION

- Kcal: 320
- Carbohydrates: 45g
- Sugars: 8g
- Fiber: 10g
- Protein: 12g
- Total Fats: 12g
- Saturated Fats: 2g
- Monounsaturated Fats: 7g
- Polyunsaturated Fats: 2g
- Sodium: 400mg

Zucchini and Corn Sauté with Basil

1. **Prep Ingredients (2 minutes)** (Slice zucchinis, mince garlic, and chop fresh basil. Preparing these ingredients first ensures a smooth cooking process. Fresh basil adds a fragrant aroma, while garlic enhances flavor, both important for creating a dish that is not only healthy but also appealing to the palate.)
2. **Heat the Oil (1 minute)** (Heat olive oil in a large skillet over medium heat. Olive oil is chosen for its health benefits, including monounsaturated fats, which are beneficial for heart health, especially important for individuals with type 2 diabetes.)
3. **Sauté Garlic and Zucchini (3 minutes)** (Add minced garlic to the skillet, sautéing briefly until fragrant, then add the sliced zucchini. Sautéing the zucchini until it begins to soften brings out its natural sweetness, complementing the garlic's flavor.)
4. **Add Corn and Season (2 minutes)** (Introduce the corn kernels to the skillet, cooking until they're heated through. Season with salt and black pepper, adjusting to taste. This step infuses the dish with a sweet and savory contrast, enhancing the overall flavor profile.)
5. **Finish with Basil and Lemon (2 minutes)** (Stir in chopped fresh basil and drizzle with lemon juice before serving. The basil adds a fresh, aromatic finish, while the lemon juice provides a bright acidity that elevates the dish, making it a refreshing and nutritious option for managing diabetes.)

INGREDIENTS

- 2 medium zucchinis, sliced (500g)
- 1 cup (150g) corn kernels, fresh or frozen
- 1 tablespoon (15ml) olive oil
- 2 cloves garlic, minced (10g)
- 1/4 cup (10g) fresh basil, chopped
- Salt to taste (minimal)
- 1/4 teaspoon (1g) black pepper
- 1 tablespoon (15ml) lemon juice

NUTRITION

- Kcal: 180
- Carbohydrates: 25g
- Sugars: 8g
- Fiber: 5g
- Protein: 5g
- Total Fats: 8g
- Saturated Fats: 1g
- Monounsaturated Fats: 5g
- Polyunsaturated Fats: 1g
- Sodium: 150mg

Vegan Pesto and Tomato Toast

1. **Toast the Bread (2 minutes)** (Place the whole grain bread slices in a toaster until crispy and golden. Whole grain bread is chosen for its high fiber content, which is beneficial for blood sugar management, providing a nutritious base for the toppings.)
2. **Spread Pesto (2 minutes)** (Spread the vegan pesto evenly over the toasted bread slices. Vegan pesto is rich in healthy fats from nuts and olive oil, making it a heart-healthy choice that adds flavor and moisture to the toast without using dairy products.)
3. **Add Tomato Slices (2 minutes)** (Layer the tomato slices on top of the pesto. Tomatoes are low in calories but high in vitamins and antioxidants, offering a juicy, fresh contrast to the rich pesto while adding minimal sugar to the dish.)
4. **Top with Arugula and Vinegar (2 minutes)** (Add a handful of arugula on top of the tomatoes and drizzle with balsamic vinegar. The peppery arugula and the sweet acidity of the vinegar enhance the toast with complex flavors and additional nutrients.)
5. **Season and Serve (2 minutes)** (Season the assembled toast with a pinch of salt and black pepper to taste. This final touch balances the flavors, making the vegan pesto and tomato toast a delicious and nutritious meal suitable for managing diabetes.)

INGREDIENTS

- 4 slices of whole grain bread (140g)
- 1/2 cup (120g) vegan pesto
- 2 medium tomatoes, sliced (180g)
- 1/4 cup (30g) arugula
- 1 tablespoon (15ml) balsamic vinegar
- Salt to taste (minimal)
- Black pepper to taste (1g)

NUTRITION

- Kcal: 350
- Carbohydrates: 40g
- Sugars: 6g
- Fiber: 8g
- Protein: 12g
- Total Fats: 18g
- Saturated Fats: 3g
- Monounsaturated Fats: 8g
- Polyunsaturated Fats: 5g
- Sodium: 480mg

Spinach and Mushroom Quesadillas

1. **Prep Ingredients (2 minutes)** (Slice the mushrooms and mince the garlic. Preparing your ingredients first streamlines the cooking process. Fresh spinach is rich in vitamins and fiber, mushrooms add umami, and garlic enhances flavor, making for a nutritious and delicious quesadilla filling.)
2. **Sauté Mushrooms and Garlic (2 minutes)** (Heat olive oil in a pan over medium heat. Add garlic and mushrooms, sautéing until the mushrooms are soft and golden. Olive oil provides healthy fats, and sautéing mushrooms brings out their natural flavors, complementing the mild garlic.)
3. **Add Spinach (2 minutes)** (Add spinach to the pan, cooking until it wilts. This step not only adds a serving of greens rich in nutrients and fiber but also introduces moisture and texture, making the filling more cohesive and flavorful.)
4. **Assemble Quesadillas (2 minutes)** (Spread the mushroom and spinach mixture on half of each tortilla, sprinkle with cheese, and fold. The cheese adds calcium and protein, while whole wheat tortillas offer a source of complex carbohydrates, fiber, and nutrients beneficial for blood sugar control.)
5. **Cook Quesadillas (2 minutes)** (Cook the quesadillas in a pan until golden brown on both sides and the cheese melts. This final cooking step melds the flavors together and adds a crispy texture to the tortillas, making the quesadillas irresistibly delicious and satisfying.)

INGREDIENTS

- 4 whole wheat tortillas (200g)
- 1 cup (225g) fresh spinach
- 1 cup (150g) sliced mushrooms
- 1/2 cup (56g) shredded low-fat cheese
- 1 tablespoon (15ml) olive oil
- 1 clove garlic, minced (5g)
- Salt to taste (minimal)
- 1/4 teaspoon (1g) black pepper

NUTRITION

- Kcal: 320
- Carbohydrates: 35g
- Sugars: 3g
- Fiber: 6g
- Protein: 15g
- Total Fats: 16g
- Saturated Fats: 4g
- Monounsaturated Fats: 8g
- Polyunsaturated Fats: 2g
- Sodium: 450mg

Edamame Salad with Sesame Ginger Dressing

1. **Prep Vegetables (2 minutes)** (Shred the carrot and slice the red cabbage thinly. Preparing the vegetables ensures they're ready to absorb the flavors of the dressing, making the salad vibrant and nutrient-rich, ideal for managing blood sugar levels in type 2 diabetes.)
2. **Mix Dressing (2 minutes)** (Whisk together sesame oil, soy sauce, rice vinegar, and grated ginger in a bowl. This sesame ginger dressing combines healthy fats with bold flavors, enhancing the salad's appeal without adding excessive sugars or sodium, crucial for a diabetic-friendly diet.)
3. **Combine Salad Ingredients (2 minutes)** (In a large bowl, mix the cooked edamame, shredded carrot, and sliced red cabbage. These ingredients offer a blend of protein, fiber, vitamins, and antioxidants, supporting overall health and blood sugar management in type 2 diabetes.)
4. **Toss with Dressing (2 minutes)** (Pour the dressing over the salad mixture and toss to coat evenly. This step ensures each component of the salad is flavored with the aromatic and tangy sesame ginger dressing, making the salad a delicious and healthful choice.)
5. **Garnish and Serve (2 minutes)** (Sprinkle sesame seeds over the salad, season with minimal salt and black pepper to taste, and serve. The sesame seeds add a nutty flavor and a crunchy texture, completing the dish with an additional layer of taste and nutrition.)

INGREDIENTS

- 1 cup (150g) edamame, shelled and cooked
- 1/2 cup (50g) shredded carrot
- 1/2 cup (50g) red cabbage, thinly sliced
- 2 tablespoons (30ml) sesame oil
- 1 tablespoon (15ml) soy sauce (low sodium)
- 1 tablespoon (15ml) rice vinegar
- 1 teaspoon (5ml) ginger, freshly grated
- 1 teaspoon (5g) sesame seeds
- Salt to taste (minimal)
- Black pepper to taste (1g)

NUTRITION

- Kcal: 250
- Carbohydrates: 15g
- Sugars: 4g
- Fiber: 5g
- Protein: 10g
- Total Fats: 18g
- Saturated Fats: 3g
- Monounsaturated Fats: 7g
- Polyunsaturated Fats: 7g
- Sodium: 300mg

Steamed Green Beans with Lemon Zest

1. **Prep Green Beans (2 minutes)** (Trim the green beans, removing any tough ends. This step ensures that all parts of the beans are tender and pleasant to eat, making them a perfect, healthful side dish for managing blood sugar levels in type 2 diabetes.)
2. **Steam Green Beans (3 minutes)** (Steam the green beans until they are just tender but still crisp. Steaming preserves the nutrients and natural flavors of the green beans, making them not only delicious but also packed with vitamins and fiber beneficial for diabetes management.)
3. **Prepare Lemon Zest (2 minutes)** (Zest one lemon, ensuring to avoid the bitter white pith beneath the yellow skin. Lemon zest adds a vibrant flavor and aroma to the dish, enhancing its appeal without adding significant calories or sugar.)
4. **Toss with Olive Oil and Lemon (2 minutes)** (Toss the steamed green beans with olive oil, lemon zest, and lemon juice. This combination brings a bright, fresh flavor to the beans, making them a flavorful addition to any meal, especially for those managing type 2 diabetes.)
5. **Season and Serve (1 minute)** (Season with minimal salt and black pepper to taste, then serve. This final step enhances the natural flavors of the dish, making the green beans a delightful, nutritious side that's both diabetes-friendly and heart-healthy.)

INGREDIENTS

- 2 cups (200g) fresh green beans, trimmed
- 1 tablespoon (15ml) olive oil
- Zest of 1 lemon (5g)
- 1 tablespoon (15ml) lemon juice
- Salt to taste (minimal)
- Black pepper to taste (1g)

NUTRITION

- Kcal: 100
- Carbohydrates: 8g
- Sugars: 4g
- Fiber: 4g
- Protein: 2g
- Total Fats: 7g
- Saturated Fats: 1g
- Monounsaturated Fats: 5g
- Polyunsaturated Fats: 1g
- Sodium: 150mg

Quick Pickled Cucumber Salad

1. **Slice Cucumbers (2 minutes)** (Thinly slice the cucumbers. This increases the surface area, allowing the pickling liquid to better penetrate the cucumbers, enhancing their flavor and making them a refreshing, low-calorie snack ideal for managing blood sugar levels.)
2. **Mix Pickling Liquid (2 minutes)** (Combine apple cider vinegar, water, sugar substitute, salt, and black pepper in a bowl. This mixture provides the tangy base for the quick pickle, offering a balance of flavors without adding excessive calories or sugar, crucial for a diabetes-friendly diet.)
3. **Add Cucumbers to Liquid (2 minutes)** (Add the sliced cucumbers to the pickling liquid, ensuring they are fully submerged. This allows the cucumbers to absorb the flavors, becoming tangy and slightly sweet, a process that enhances their nutritional value without raising blood sugar levels significantly.)
4. **Marinate (2 minutes)** (Let the cucumbers marinate in the liquid for a few minutes, stirring occasionally. This short marinating time is sufficient for the cucumbers to begin pickling, making them flavorful and crisp, perfect for a quick, healthy salad.)
5. **Garnish and Serve (2 minutes)** (Sprinkle with fresh dill before serving. The dill adds a fresh, herby flavor that complements the tanginess of the pickled cucumbers, completing the dish with a burst of flavor and a touch of green, enhancing its visual and nutritional appeal.)

INGREDIENTS

- 2 medium cucumbers, thinly sliced (500g)
- 1/4 cup (60ml) apple cider vinegar
- 1 tablespoon (15ml) water
- 1 tablespoon (15g) sugar substitute (suitable for diabetics)
- 1/2 teaspoon (2.5g) salt
- 1/4 teaspoon (1g) black pepper
- 1 tablespoon (15ml) fresh dill, chopped

NUTRITION

- Kcal: 50
- Carbohydrates: 8g
- Sugars: 4g (from cucumbers, natural sugars)
- Fiber: 2g
- Protein: 2g
- Total Fats: 0g
- Saturated Fats: 0g
- Monounsaturated Fats: 0g
- Polyunsaturated Fats: 0g
- Sodium: 590mg

Sautéed Kale with Garlic and Olive Oil

1. **Prep Kale (2 minutes)** (Wash and chop the kale, removing the tough stems. This ensures the kale is clean and the leaves are tender and easy to eat, making them a nutritious base for this dish, rich in vitamins and minerals beneficial for managing blood sugar levels.)
2. **Heat Olive Oil (1 minute)** (Heat olive oil in a large skillet over medium heat. Olive oil is chosen for its heart-healthy fats and its ability to cook the kale evenly without burning, providing a flavorful and nutritious component to the dish.)
3. **Sauté Garlic (2 minutes)** (Add minced garlic to the skillet, sautéing until fragrant. Garlic adds a robust flavor to the kale, enhancing the overall taste of the dish while also offering health benefits, such as improving heart health and supporting immune function.)
4. **Cook Kale (3 minutes)** (Add the kale to the skillet, seasoning with salt and pepper. Sauté until the kale is wilted and tender but still vibrant green. This method preserves the kale's nutrients and texture, making it more palatable and beneficial for those with diabetes.)
5. **Finish with Lemon (2 minutes)** (Drizzle lemon juice over the cooked kale and toss to combine. The lemon juice adds a bright, acidic finish that elevates the flavors of the dish, making it a delicious, low-carb side that complements a variety of main courses.)

INGREDIENTS

- 4 cups (120g) kale, stems removed and leaves chopped
- 2 tablespoons (30ml) olive oil
- 2 cloves garlic, minced (10g)
- Salt to taste (minimal)
- 1/4 teaspoon (1g) black pepper
- 1 tablespoon (15ml) lemon juice

NUTRITION

- Kcal: 150
- Carbohydrates: 10g
- Sugars: 0g
- Fiber: 2g
- Protein: 3g
- Total Fats: 14g
- Saturated Fats: 2g
- Monounsaturated Fats: 10g
- Polyunsaturated Fats: 2g
- Sodium: 200mg

Microwave Steamed Asparagus

1. **Prep Asparagus (2 minutes)** (Trim the woody ends from the asparagus. This ensures that every bite is tender and flavorful, making the asparagus a delicious, nutrient-dense vegetable that's high in fiber and vitamins, perfect for managing blood sugar levels in type 2 diabetes.)
2. **Arrange for Microwaving (2 minutes)** (Place the asparagus in a microwave-safe dish and add water. The water will steam the asparagus in the microwave, cooking it quickly while preserving its nutrients and green color, making it a healthy and convenient cooking method for a diabetes-friendly diet.)
3. **Microwave Asparagus (3 minutes)** (Cover the dish with plastic wrap and microwave on high for 3 minutes. This quick steaming method locks in flavors and nutrients, resulting in perfectly tender asparagus that's ideal for a quick, healthy side dish.)
4. **Season Asparagus (2 minutes)** (Drizzle olive oil over the cooked asparagus. Season with salt and black pepper, then toss to coat evenly. Olive oil adds a rich, monounsaturated fat that's heart-healthy, while the seasonings enhance the natural flavor of the asparagus without adding unnecessary sugars or sodium.)
5. **Finish with Lemon (1 minute)** (Sprinkle lemon juice over the asparagus before serving. The lemon juice adds a fresh, zesty finish that brightens the dish, making it a flavorful, low-carb side that complements any main course, especially for those managing diabetes.)

INGREDIENTS

- 1 pound (450g) fresh asparagus, trimmed
- 2 tablespoons (30ml) water
- 1 tablespoon (15ml) olive oil
- Salt to taste (minimal)
- 1/4 teaspoon (1g) black pepper
- 1 teaspoon (5ml) lemon juice

NUTRITION

- Kcal: 60
- Carbohydrates: 4g
- Sugars: 2g
- Fiber: 2g
- Protein: 2g
- Total Fats: 4g
- Saturated Fats: 0.5g
- Monounsaturated Fats: 3g
- Polyunsaturated Fats: 0.5g
- Sodium: 200mg

Tomato and Onion Salad with Olive Oil

1. **Slice Tomatoes and Onion (2 minutes)** (Slice the tomatoes and onion thinly. This preparation method enhances the salad's texture and ensures the flavors meld well together. Tomatoes are a good source of vitamins C and K, important for overall health, while onions add a sharp contrast.)
2. **Arrange on Plate (2 minutes)** (Arrange the tomato and onion slices on a serving plate, alternating for visual appeal. This step not only makes the dish visually appealing but also allows for an even distribution of flavors with each bite, crucial for a satisfying eating experience.)
3. **Drizzle Dressing (2 minutes)** (Whisk together olive oil and balsamic vinegar, then drizzle over the tomatoes and onions. The olive oil adds healthy fats, while the balsamic vinegar provides a sweet and tangy flavor, enhancing the natural sweetness of the tomatoes.)
4. **Season Salad (2 minutes)** (Season the salad with minimal salt and black pepper. This enhances the flavors without overpowering the natural taste of the ingredients, ensuring the dish remains healthy and suitable for people managing type 2 diabetes.)
5. **Garnish with Basil (2 minutes)**
(Sprinkle chopped fresh basil over the top before serving. Basil adds a fresh, aromatic element to the salad, tying all the flavors together and adding a burst of color, making the dish both flavorful and visually appealing.)

INGREDIENTS

- 2 large tomatoes, sliced (400g)
- 1 medium red onion, thinly sliced (150g)
- 2 tablespoons (30ml) olive oil
- 1 tablespoon (15ml) balsamic vinegar
- Salt to taste (minimal)
- 1/4 teaspoon (1g) black pepper
- 1 tablespoon (15g) fresh basil, chopped

NUTRITION

- **Kcal: 140**
- **Carbohydrates: 12g**
- **Sugars: 8g**
- **Fiber: 3g**
- **Protein: 2g**
- **Total Fats: 10g**
- **Saturated Fats: 1.5g**
- **Monounsaturated Fats: 7g**
- **Polyunsaturated Fats: 1.5g**
- **Sodium: 200mg**

Roasted Red Pepper and Walnut Dip

1. **Prepare Ingredients (2 minutes)** (Measure and prepare all ingredients. This includes draining the roasted red peppers, measuring walnuts, peeling garlic, and squeezing lemon juice. Preparing ingredients beforehand streamlines the cooking process, ensuring everything is ready for a quick and efficient blend.)
2. **Blend Peppers and Walnuts (2 minutes)** (Place roasted red peppers, walnuts, and garlic in a food processor. These ingredients form the base of the dip, combining sweet, nutty, and savory flavors. The walnuts add texture and healthy fats, making this dip not only delicious but also nutritious for managing diabetes.)
3. **Add Liquids and Spices (2 minutes)** (To the food processor, add olive oil, lemon juice, ground cumin, and smoked paprika. Olive oil enhances the dip's richness, lemon juice adds brightness, and the spices introduce warmth and depth, creating a complex flavor profile that's both enticing and diabetic-friendly.)
4. **Process to Desired Consistency (2 minutes)** (Blend until the mixture reaches your desired consistency, whether smooth or slightly chunky. This step allows for personal preference in texture, ensuring the dip is appealing to various tastes while maintaining its healthful properties.)
5. **Season and Serve (2 minutes)** (Taste and adjust seasoning with minimal salt, if necessary. The final seasoning step ensures the dip has a balanced flavor profile. Serve immediately or chill for later. This versatile dip can complement a variety of dishes, providing a flavorful and health-conscious option for those managing diabetes.)

INGREDIENTS

- 1 cup (150g) roasted red peppers, drained
- 1/2 cup (60g) walnuts
- 1 clove garlic (5g)
- 2 tablespoons (30ml) olive oil
- 1 tablespoon (15ml) lemon juice
- 1/2 teaspoon (2.5g) ground cumin
- Salt to taste (minimal)
- 1/4 teaspoon (1g) smoked paprika

NUTRITION

- Kcal: 300
- Carbohydrates: 8g
- Sugars: 4g
- Fiber: 3g
- Protein: 4g
- Total Fats: 28g
- Saturated Fats: 3g
- Monounsaturated Fats: 15g
- Polyunsaturated Fats: 10g
- Sodium: 400mg

Sweet Corn and Black Bean Salad

1. **Combine Corn and Beans (2 minutes)** (Mix cooked sweet corn and black beans in a bowl. These ingredients form the hearty base of the salad, providing a rich source of fiber and protein that is crucial for blood sugar management in type 2 diabetes.)
2. **Add Tomatoes and Onion (2 minutes)** (Stir in diced tomato and chopped red onion. The fresh vegetables add a burst of flavor and a wealth of vitamins, enhancing the nutritional profile of the salad while keeping it light and refreshing.)
3. **Season with Lime and Spices (2 minutes)** (Drizzle lime juice and olive oil over the salad. Add ground cumin and salt, then toss to combine. The dressing introduces a zesty, tangy flavor that complements the sweetness of the corn and the earthiness of the beans.)
4. **Garnish with Cilantro (2 minutes)** (Sprinkle chopped cilantro over the salad. The cilantro adds a fresh, herbal note that brightens the entire dish, tying all the flavors together in a harmonious blend.)
5. **Chill and Serve (2 minutes)** (Chill the salad for a few minutes before serving. This allows the flavors to meld together more fully, making the salad even more delicious. Serve as a refreshing, nutritious side dish that's both diabetes-friendly and satisfying.)

INGREDIENTS

- 1 cup (175g) cooked sweet corn
- 1 cup (170g) black beans, rinsed and drained
- 1 medium tomato, diced (150g)
- 1/4 cup (40g) red onion, finely chopped
- 2 tablespoons (30ml) lime juice
- 1 tablespoon (15ml) olive oil
- 1/4 teaspoon (1g) ground cumin
- Salt to taste (minimal)
- 1/4 cup (15g) fresh cilantro, chopped

NUTRITION

- Kcal: 220
- Carbohydrates: 35g
- Sugars: 6g
- Fiber: 10g
- Protein: 8g
- Total Fats: 7g
- Saturated Fats: 1g
- Monounsaturated Fats: 4g
- Polyunsaturated Fats: 1g
- Sodium: 300mg

Garlic and Herb Microwave-Steamed Carrots

1. **Prep the Ingredients (2 minutes)** (Wash and slice carrots into uniform pieces for even cooking. Mince the garlic clove. Measure olive oil, thyme, rosemary, salt, and pepper. Preparing ingredients before cooking simplifies the process and ensures everything is ready.)
2. **Season the Carrots (2 minutes)** (In a microwave-safe dish, combine carrots, minced garlic, olive oil, thyme, rosemary, salt, and pepper. Toss everything together to ensure the carrots are evenly coated with the seasoning. This step infuses the carrots with flavor.)
3. **Microwave Steaming (4 minutes)** (Cover the dish with a microwave-safe lid or plastic wrap. Microwave on high for 4 minutes. The steam trapped inside will cook the carrots, making them tender while retaining their nutrients.)
4. **Check and Stir (1 minute)** (Carefully remove the dish from the microwave. Stir the carrots to ensure they're evenly cooked. Test for tenderness; if needed, microwave for an additional minute. Adjust seasoning if necessary.)
5. **Serve (1 minute)** (Transfer the steamed carrots to a serving plate. Garnish with a sprig of thyme or rosemary for a touch of color and extra flavor. Enjoy this healthy, diabetic-friendly side dish while hot.)

INGREDIENTS

- 1 cup (~240g) Carrots
- 1 clove (~5g) Garlic
- 1 tablespoon (~15ml) Olive oil
- 1 teaspoon (~5g) Fresh thyme
- 1 teaspoon (~5g) Fresh rosemary
- 1/4 teaspoon (~1.25g) Salt
- 1/4 teaspoon (~1.25g) Black pepper

NUTRITION

- **Kcal:** 120 Kcal
- **Carbohydrates:** 15g
- **Sugars:** 7g
- **Fiber:** 4g
- **Protein:** 1g
- **Total Fats:** 7g
- **Saturated Fats:** 1g
- **Monounsaturated Fats:** 5g
- **Polyunsaturated Fats:** 1g
- **Sodium:** 300mg

Quick Tomato Basil Soup

1. **Combine Ingredients (2 minutes)** Place diced tomatoes, vegetable broth, chopped basil, minced garlic, olive oil, salt, and pepper in a large microwave-safe bowl. Stirring ensures flavors meld together, creating a harmonious base for the soup.
2. **Microwave (5 minutes)** Cover the bowl with a microwave-safe lid or vented plastic wrap. Microwave on high until the soup is hot and aromatic. This quick cooking method preserves the bright flavors of the tomatoes and basil.
3. **Blend (2 minutes)** Carefully transfer the soup to a blender. Blend until smooth, adjusting the texture to your liking. This step enhances the soup's creamy consistency while maintaining a chunky texture if desired.
4. **Taste and Adjust (0.5 minutes)** Sample the soup. Adjust seasoning with additional salt and pepper if needed. This crucial step ensures the soup meets your taste preferences, balancing acidity and seasoning.
5. **Serve (0.5 minutes)** Pour soup into bowls. Garnish with a dollop of Greek yogurt and a sprinkle of fresh basil. The yogurt adds a creamy tanginess, complementing the soup's vibrant flavors.

INGREDIENTS

- 14.5 oz can (410g) Canned no-salt-added diced tomatoes
- 1 cup (240ml) Low-sodium vegetable broth
- 2 tablespoons (30g) Chopped fresh basil
- 1 teaspoon (5g) Minced garlic
- 1 teaspoon (5ml) Extra-virgin olive oil
- 1/4 teaspoon (1.25g) Salt
- 1/4 teaspoon (1.25g) Black pepper
- 2 tbsp (30g) Low-fat plain Greek yogurt

NUTRITION

- **Kcal:** 90 Kcal
- **Carbohydrates:** 13g
- **Sugars:** 8g
- **Fiber:** 3g
- **Protein:** 4g
- **Total Fats:** 3g
- **Saturated Fats:** 0.5g
- **Monounsaturated Fats:** 2g
- **Polyunsaturated Fats:** 0.5g
- **Sodium:** 200mg

Simple Miso Soup

1. **Prep Ingredients (2 minutes)** Measure water, miso paste, and prepare tofu by cubing it into bite-sized pieces. Rehydrate dried wakame in a separate bowl with a little water. Slice green onions thinly. This prepares all ingredients for quick assembly.
2. **Heat Water (2 minutes)** Pour water into a pot and heat on the stove until just before boiling. It's crucial not to boil water after adding miso to preserve its flavor and probiotics.
3. **Dissolve Miso Paste (3 minutes)** In a small bowl, dissolve miso paste with a bit of the hot water to make a slurry. Then, stir this back into the pot of hot water to ensure even distribution without clumping.
4. **Add Tofu and Wakame (2 minutes)** Add the cubed tofu and rehydrated wakame to the pot. Let them warm through without boiling the soup, maintaining the delicate flavors and nutrients of the ingredients.
5. **Serve (1 minute)** Ladle the soup into bowls and garnish with sliced green onions. Serve immediately to enjoy the soothing warmth and umami richness, perfect for a diabetic-friendly diet.

INGREDIENTS

- 4 cups (960ml) Water
- 2 tablespoons (30g) Miso paste
- 1/2 cup (125g) Tofu (firm, cubed)
- 1 tablespoon (15g) Dried wakame seaweed
- 2 tablespoons (30g) Sliced green onions

NUTRITION

- **Kcal:** 80 Kcal
- **Carbohydrates:** 7g
- **Sugars:** 2g
- **Fiber:** 2g
- **Protein:** 6g
- **Total Fats:** 3g
- **Saturated Fats:** 0.5g
- **Monounsaturated Fats:** 1g
- **Polyunsaturated Fats:** 1.5g
- **Sodium:** 900mg

Mini Frittatas with Spinach and Feta

1. **Broth Preparation (2 minutes)** Heat chicken broth in a pot over medium heat. Season with soy sauce, sesame oil, salt, and pepper. This base of the soup provides depth and umami, essential for the egg drop soup's characteristic flavor profile.
2. **Cornstarch Slurry (2 minutes)** Mix cornstarch with water in a small bowl until smooth. This slurry is key to thickening the soup slightly, giving it a silky texture that complements the soft egg ribbons.
3. **Eggs (2 minutes)** Beat eggs in a bowl. This prepares them for being streamed into the hot broth, where they will cook immediately, forming delicate, cloud-like egg ribbons that are the hallmark of egg drop soup.
4. **Combine (3 minutes)** Slowly pour the egg into the simmering broth, stirring gently with a fork to create egg ribbons. The gentle motion ensures the eggs cook in beautiful, wispy strands, enhancing the soup's visual and textural appeal.
5. **Finish and Serve (1 minute)** Stir in the cornstarch slurry until the soup slightly thickens. Serve hot, garnished with green onions. The final soup is a harmonious blend of savory flavors, with a comforting, nutritious profile perfect for those managing type 2 diabetes.

INGREDIENTS

- 4 cups (960ml) Chicken broth
- 2 large (2 eggs) Eggs
- 1 tablespoon (15g) Cornstarch
- 2 tablespoons (30ml) Water
- 2 tablespoons (30g) Green onions, chopped
- 1 teaspoon (5ml) Soy sauce
- 1 teaspoon (5ml) Sesame oil
- 1/4 teaspoon (1.25g) Salt
- 1/4 teaspoon (1.25g) Pepper

NUTRITION

- **Kcal:** 150 Kcal
- **Carbohydrates:** 8g
- **Sugars:** 2g
- **Fiber:** 0g
- **Protein:** 12g
- **Total Fats:** 8g
- **Saturated Fats:** 2g
- **Monounsaturated Fats:** 3g
- **Polyunsaturated Fats:** 3g
- **Sodium:** 900mg

Zucchini and Basil Soup

1. **Prep the Zucchini (2 minutes)** Wash and chop the zucchini into small pieces. Mince the garlic. This preparation is crucial for a smooth cooking process, ensuring that the zucchini cooks evenly and quickly absorbs the flavors of the broth and herbs.
2. **Sauté Garlic (1 minute)** Heat olive oil in a pot over medium heat. Add minced garlic, sautéing until fragrant. This step lays the flavor foundation for the soup, infusing it with the aromatic qualities of garlic without overwhelming the delicate taste of zucchini.
3. **Cook Zucchini (3 minutes)** Add chopped zucchini to the pot, seasoning with salt and pepper. Cook until slightly softened. This brief cooking time retains the zucchini's fresh flavor and nutrients, which are essential for a diabetes-friendly diet.
4. **Add Broth and Simmer (3 minutes)** Pour in vegetable broth and bring to a simmer. The broth not only cooks the zucchini further but also melds the flavors of the soup together, creating a harmonious blend that is both nutritious and flavorful.
5. **Blend and Serve (1 minute)** Remove from heat and stir in fresh basil leaves. Blend until smooth for a creamy consistency. Serve the soup hot, garnished with a basil leaf. This final step enhances the soup's fresh, herbal notes, making it a comforting and healthful dish.

INGREDIENTS

- 2 medium (500g) Zucchini
- 2 cups (480ml) Low-sodium vegetable broth
- 1/4 cup (15g) Fresh basil leaves
- 1 tablespoon (15ml) Olive oil
- 1 clove (5g) Garlic
- 1/4 teaspoon (1.25g) Salt
- 1/4 teaspoon (1.25g) Black pepper

NUTRITION

- **Kcal:** 120 Kcal
- **Carbohydrates:** 15g
- **Sugars:** 9g
- **Fiber:** 5g
- **Protein:** 3g
- **Total Fats:** 7g
- **Saturated Fats:** 1g
- **Monounsaturated Fats:** 5g
- **Polyunsaturated Fats:** 1g
- **Sodium:** 300mg

Pea and Mint Soup

1. **Heat the Broth (2 minutes)** Pour vegetable broth into a medium pot and bring to a simmer over medium heat. This step is crucial for dissolving flavors and ensuring the soup base is ready for the peas and mint, which will be added shortly.
2. **Cook the Peas (2 minutes)** Add frozen peas to the simmering broth. Cook until they are just tender but still vibrant green. The quick cooking preserves their sweet flavor and bright color, which are essential for the final appearance and taste of the soup.
3. **Add Mint (1 minute)** Stir in fresh mint leaves, torn or whole, into the pot. The mint infuses the soup with its fresh, aromatic flavor, enhancing the sweet peas with a refreshing depth that's both unexpected and delightful.
4. **Blend the Soup (4 minutes)** Carefully transfer the mixture to a blender. Blend until smooth for a creamy consistency, adjusting the texture with additional broth if needed. This step transforms the ingredients into a silky soup, marrying the flavors of pea and mint perfectly.
5. **Season and Serve (1 minute)** Return the soup to the pot. Season with salt and pepper to taste. Serve hot, drizzled with a bit of olive oil for a rich finish. The olive oil adds a smooth mouthfeel and complements the soup's freshness, making it a comforting, diabetic-friendly meal.

INGREDIENTS

- 2 cups (480g) Frozen peas
- 2 cups (480ml) Low-sodium vegetable broth
- 1/4 cup (15g) Fresh mint leaves
- 1 tablespoon (15ml) Olive oil
- 1/4 teaspoon (1.25g) Salt
- 1/4 teaspoon (1.25g) Black pepper

NUTRITION

- **Kcal:** 180 Kcal
- **Carbohydrates:** 24g
- **Sugars:** 9g
- **Fiber:** 8g
- **Protein:** 8g
- **Total Fats:** 7g
- **Saturated Fats:** 1g
- **Monounsaturated Fats:** 5g
- **Polyunsaturated Fats:** 1g
- **Sodium:** 200mg

Spicy Black Bean Soup

1. **Sauté Onions and Garlic (2 minutes)** Heat olive oil in a pot. Add chopped onions and minced garlic, cooking until softened. This foundational step layers flavors, as onions and garlic release their aromatic compounds, setting a savory base for the soup.
2. **Spice It Up (1 minute)** Stir in ground cumin and chili powder. Toasting the spices for a brief period unlocks their flavors, infusing the soup with a warm, complex depth that's both aromatic and enticing.
3. **Add Beans and Broth (3 minutes)** Incorporate black beans (with liquid) and vegetable broth. The beans offer protein and fiber, essential for blood sugar management, while the broth melds the ingredients into a cohesive, flavorful mixture.
4. **Simmer and Blend (3 minutes)** Bring to a simmer, then blend about half the soup to thicken it while keeping some beans whole for texture. This step enhances the soup's creamy consistency without diluting its robust flavors.
5. **Finish with Freshness (1 minute)** Stir in diced tomatoes, cilantro, and lime juice. This final flourish adds brightness and a hint of acidity, balancing the soup's spicy and savory notes. Serve hot, garnished with extra cilantro or a lime wedge for an added zest.

INGREDIENTS

- 1 can (425g) Canned black beans
- 2 cups (480ml) Low-sodium vegetable broth
- 1/4 cup (40g) Chopped onions
- 1 teaspoon (5g) Minced garlic
- 1/2 teaspoon (2.5g) Ground cumin
- 1 teaspoon (5g) Chili powder
- 1/2 cup (120g) Diced tomatoes
- 2 tablespoons (30g) Chopped fresh cilantro
- 1 tablespoon (15ml) Lime juice
- 1 tablespoon (15ml) Olive oil
- 1/4 teaspoon (1.25g) Salt
- 1/4 teaspoon (1.25g) Black pepper

NUTRITION

- **Kcal:** 200 Kcal
- **Carbohydrates:** 30g
- **Sugars:** 5g
- **Fiber:** 10g
- **Protein:** 12g
- **Total Fats:** 5g
- **Saturated Fats:** 1g
- **Monounsaturated Fats:** 3g
- **Polyunsaturated Fats:** 1g
- **Sodium:** 500mg

Shrimp Corn Soup

1. **Sauté Onions and Garlic (2 minutes)** Heat olive oil in a pot over medium heat. Add onions and garlic, sautéing until translucent. This step builds a flavorful foundation, enhancing the soup with aromatic undertones crucial for a rich, layered taste.
2. **Add Shrimp (2 minutes)** Introduce shrimp to the pot, cooking until they turn pink. This quick cook ensures the shrimp remain tender and succulent, imbuing the soup with their distinct, briny flavor, which complements the sweetness of the corn.
3. **Combine Corn and Broth (3 minutes)** Add frozen corn and vegetable broth, bringing to a simmer. The corn lends a sweet pop to the soup, while the broth melds the flavors together into a cohesive, comforting blend.
4. **Finish with Cream (2 minutes)** Stir in light cream, warming through without boiling. The cream adds a velvety texture and a touch of richness, rounding out the flavors without overpowering the delicate balance of the soup.
5. **Season and Garnish (1 minute)** Season with salt and pepper. Serve the soup garnished with fresh parsley. This final touch introduces a fresh, herbaceous element, elevating the soup with a burst of color and flavor, ready to be savored.

INGREDIENTS

- 8 ounces (225g) Raw shrimp, peeled and deveined
- 1 cup (240g) Frozen corn kernels
- 2 cups (480ml) Low-sodium vegetable broth
- 1/4 cup (60ml) Light cream
- 1/4 cup (40g) Chopped onions
- 1 teaspoon (5g) Minced garlic
- 1 tablespoon (15ml) Olive oil
- 1/4 teaspoon (1.25g) Salt
- 1/4 teaspoon (1.25g) Black pepper
- 1 tablespoon (15g) Chopped fresh parsley

NUTRITION

- **Kcal:** 250 Kcal
- **Carbohydrates:** 20g
- **Sugars:** 5g
- **Fiber:** 2g
- **Protein:** 25g
- **Total Fats:** 8g
- **Saturated Fats:** 3g
- **Monounsaturated Fats:** 4g
- **Polyunsaturated Fats:** 1g
- **Sodium:** 300mg

Greek Yogurt with Honey and Cinnamon

1. **Prepare the Ingredients (2 minutes)** Measure out the Greek yogurt, honey, ground cinnamon, and, if using, chop the walnuts. Preparing these ingredients beforehand makes the assembly process smoother and ensures even distribution of flavors throughout the dish.
2. **Mix Yogurt and Cinnamon (2 minutes)** Combine the Greek yogurt with the ground cinnamon in a bowl. Stirring thoroughly ensures the cinnamon is evenly distributed, infusing the yogurt with its warm, aromatic flavor, which complements the creamy texture of the yogurt.
3. **Add Honey (1 minute)** Drizzle the honey over the yogurt mixture. Honey not only adds a natural sweetness but also enhances the overall flavor profile, creating a delightful contrast with the tanginess of the Greek yogurt.
4. **Garnish with Walnuts (2 minutes)** Sprinkle the chopped walnuts on top of the yogurt. This optional step adds a crunchy texture and nutty flavor, enriching the dish with additional healthy fats and protein, making it a more satisfying snack or dessert.
5. **Serve (3 minutes)** Divide the yogurt mixture into serving bowls. This final step presents the dish beautifully, allowing the cinnamon and honey to shine as the main flavors, with the optional walnuts providing an extra layer of taste and texture. Enjoy this simple, nutritious, and diabetic-friendly treat.

INGREDIENTS

- 1 cup (245g) Low-fat Greek yogurt
- 2 tablespoons (30ml) Honey
- 1/2 teaspoon (2.5g) Ground cinnamon
- 2 tablespoons (30g) Walnuts, chopped (optional)

NUTRITION

- **Kcal:** 150 Kcal
- **Carbohydrates:** 18g
- **Sugars:** 17g (natural sugars from honey and lactose in yogurt)
- **Fiber:** 0g (1g if walnuts are included)
- **Protein:** 12g
- **Total Fats:** 4g (increase to 7g with walnuts)
- **Saturated Fats:** 1g
- **Monounsaturated Fats:** 1g (increase with walnuts)
- **Polyunsaturated Fats:** 2g (increase with walnuts)
- **Sodium:** 55mg

Dark Chocolate-Dipped Strawberries

1. **Melt Chocolate (3 minutes)** Break dark chocolate into pieces and melt in a microwave-safe bowl, checking every 30 seconds to avoid burning. Melting chocolate gently ensures it's smooth and silky, perfect for coating the strawberries, enriching them with a decadent layer of flavor.
2. **Prepare Strawberries (2 minutes)** Wash and dry strawberries thoroughly. Ensuring strawberries are dry is crucial for the chocolate to adhere properly, creating a seamless coating that envelops the fruit in a rich, luscious embrace.
3. **Dip Strawberries (2 minutes)** Hold strawberries by the stem and dip into melted chocolate, swirling to coat evenly. This step is where the magic happens, transforming the humble strawberry into a gourmet treat, the chocolate shell encasing the juicy fruit in a delightful contrast of flavors and textures.
4. **Cool (2 minutes)** Place chocolate-dipped strawberries on a parchment-lined tray. Cooling allows the chocolate to set, forming a crisp shell that snaps with each bite, revealing the succulent, sweet strawberry within, a symphony of textures and tastes in harmony.
5. **Garnish (1 minute)** Sprinkle with a pinch of sea salt, if desired. The optional sea salt garnish elevates the dish, adding a subtle crunch and enhancing the chocolate's deep flavors, striking a balance between sweet and savory, a culinary delight in every bite.

INGREDIENTS

- 4 ounces (115g) Dark chocolate (70% or higher)
- 8 large (8 strawberries) Fresh strawberries
- A pinch (0.5g) Sea salt (optional)

NUTRITION

- **Kcal:** 200 Kcal
- **Carbohydrates:** 20g
- **Sugars:** 15g
- **Fiber:** 3g
- **Protein:** 2g
- **Total Fats:** 12g
- **Saturated Fats:** 7g
- **Monounsaturated Fats:** 3g
- **Polyunsaturated Fats:** 1g
- **Sodium:** 50mg

Ricotta and Honey with Sliced Almonds

1. **Prepare Ingredients (2 minutes)** Measure ricotta cheese, honey, sliced almonds, and ground cinnamon. Having ingredients prepared ensures the assembly process is efficient and smooth, allowing for even distribution of flavors throughout the dish.
2. **Layer Ricotta (2 minutes)** Spoon ricotta cheese into serving bowls. Layering the cheese as the base provides a creamy, mild foundation that perfectly complements the sweetness of the honey and the nutty crunch of almonds.
3. **Drizzle Honey (2 minutes)** Drizzle honey evenly over the ricotta. The honey not only adds a natural sweetness but also enhances the ricotta's flavor, creating a delightful contrast with its tangy profile. **Sprinkle Almonds and Cinnamon (2 minutes)**
4. Top with sliced almonds and a dusting of ground cinnamon. This step introduces texture and a warm spice note, enriching the dish with a complex flavor palette and making it a visually appealing treat.
5. **Serve (2 minutes)** Serve immediately to enjoy the contrasting textures and flavors. This final step presents the dish beautifully, allowing the individual components to shine, offering a simple yet elegant dessert or snack that's both nutritious and diabetic-friendly.

INGREDIENTS

- 1 cup (240g) Part-skim ricotta cheese
- 2 tablespoons (30ml) Honey
- 2 tablespoons (30g) Sliced almonds
- 1/2 teaspoon (2.5g) Ground cinnamon

NUTRITION

- **Kcal:** 250 Kcal
- **Carbohydrates:** 18g
- **Sugars:** 16g
- **Fiber:** 1g
- **Protein:** 14g
- **Total Fats:** 12g
- **Saturated Fats:** 5g
- **Monounsaturated Fats:** 4g
- **Polyunsaturated Fats:** 2g
- **Sodium:** 180mg

Fresh Fruit Salad with Mint

1. **Chop and Segment Fruits (2 minutes)** Prepare the apple, orange, strawberries, and banana by chopping and segmenting them into bite-sized pieces. This ensures a variety of textures and flavors in every bite, making the salad both visually appealing and deliciously refreshing.
2. **Mix Fruits (2 minutes)** In a large bowl, gently toss the prepared fruits together. This step is essential for evenly distributing the different flavors and textures, ensuring that each serving of the salad is uniformly delicious and colorful.
3. **Add Mint and Lemon Juice (2 minutes)** Sprinkle chopped mint leaves over the fruit and drizzle with lemon juice. The mint adds a fresh, aromatic flavor, while the lemon juice provides a bright, tangy contrast that enhances the natural sweetness of the fruits.
4. **Drizzle Honey (Optional) (2 minutes)** If using, lightly drizzle honey over the salad. This optional step introduces an additional layer of sweetness, complementing the fruits' flavors without overpowering them, making the salad even more enticing.
5. **Serve (2 minutes)** Divide the salad into serving bowls. This final touch presents the dish beautifully, allowing the vibrant colors, varied textures, and harmonious flavors of the fruits, mint, and optional honey to shine through, creating a simple yet elegant dessert or snack.

INGREDIENTS

- 1 medium (180g) Apple, chopped
- 1 medium (130g) Orange, segmented
- 1 cup (150g) Strawberries, halved
- 1 medium (120g) Banana, sliced
- 1 tablespoon (5g) Fresh mint leaves, chopped
- 1 tablespoon (15ml) Lemon juice
- 1 teaspoon (5ml) Honey (optional)

NUTRITION

- **Kcal:** 180 Kcal
- **Carbohydrates:** 45g
- **Sugars:** 30g natural sugars
- **Fiber:** 6g
- **Protein:** 2g
- **Total Fats:** 0.5g
- **Saturated Fats:** 0g
- **Monounsaturated Fats:** 0g
- **Polyunsaturated Fats:** 0g
- **Sodium:** 5mg

Frozen Blueberries with a Drizzle of Cream

1. **Measure Ingredients (2 minutes)** Measure out the frozen blueberries and heavy cream. Precise measurement ensures that the portion sizes are appropriate for a balanced, diabetic-friendly treat, emphasizing portion control and nutritional balance.
2. **Arrange Blueberries (2 minutes)** Place frozen blueberries in serving bowls. Using frozen blueberries provides a refreshing and cool texture, perfect for a quick dessert or snack, offering a delightful contrast when paired with cream.
3. **Drizzle Cream (2 minutes)** Drizzle heavy cream over the blueberries evenly. The cream adds a luxurious texture and richness to the dessert, creating a simple yet indulgent treat that's easy to prepare and enjoy.
4. **Garnish (Optional) (2 minutes)** Optionally, garnish with a mint leaf or a sprinkle of cinnamon for added flavor and visual appeal. This step introduces an extra layer of taste and a dash of color, enhancing the overall presentation of the dish.
5. **Serve Immediately (2 minutes)** Serve the dessert immediately to enjoy the crisp, chilled texture of the blueberries contrasted with the smooth cream. This quick and easy dessert combines convenience with deliciousness, suitable for a diabetes-friendly diet.

INGREDIENTS

- 1 cup (240g) Frozen blueberries
- 2 tablespoons (30ml) Heavy cream

NUTRITION

- **Kcal**: 120 Kcal
- **Carbohydrates**: 18g
- **Sugars**: 15g (natural sugars from blueberries)
- **Fiber**: 4g
- **Protein**: 1g
- **Total Fats**: 6g
- **Saturated Fats**: 4g
- **Monounsaturated Fats**: 1.5g
- **Polyunsaturated Fats**: 0.5g
- **Sodium**: 20mg

Mango and Coconut Rice Paper Rolls

1. **Hydrate Rice Paper (2 minutes)** Soak rice paper sheets in warm water for about 20-30 seconds until soft. This crucial step makes them pliable, allowing for easy wrapping of the fillings without breaking, serving as the perfect envelope for the vibrant fillings.
2. **Arrange Fillings (2 minutes)** Lay out soaked rice paper. Place mango, avocado, optional shrimp, coconut flakes, and mint leaves on one edge. The distribution of fillings ensures every bite is packed with flavor, texture, and nutrition, balancing sweet, savory, and fresh notes.
3. **Roll Tightly (2 minutes)** Carefully roll the rice paper, tucking in the sides to enclose the fillings. Rolling tightly is key to securing the fillings, ensuring the rolls are compact and the ingredients meld harmoniously, offering a cohesive taste experience.
4. **Mix Sauce (2 minutes)** Whisk together lime juice and optional fish sauce. This zesty and savory sauce complements the rolls, adding a tangy and umami flavor that elevates the overall dish, tying together the diverse ingredients with its bright notes.
5. **Serve (2 minutes)** Cut rolls in half, if desired, and serve with the sauce. Presenting the rolls showcases the beautiful cross-section of colors and textures, inviting diners to enjoy a fresh, flavorful, and diabetes-friendly meal that delights the senses.

INGREDIENTS

- 4 sheets Rice paper sheets
- 1/2 cup (120g) Mango, thinly sliced
- 1/2 cup (120g) Cooked shrimp, halved (optional)
- 1/2 medium (100g) Avocado, thinly sliced
- 2 tablespoons (15g) Coconut flakes
- 1/4 cup (15g) Fresh mint leaves
- 1 tablespoon (15ml) Lime juice
- 1 teaspoon (5ml) Fish sauce (optional)

NUTRITION

- **Kcal:** 200 Kcal
- **Carbohydrates:** 25g
- **Sugars:** 12g
- **Fiber:** 5g
- **Protein:** 8g (with shrimp) / 2g (without shrimp)
- **Total Fats:** 8g
- **Saturated Fats:** 3g
- **Monounsaturated Fats:** 2g
- **Polyunsaturated Fats:** 1g
- **Sodium:** 150mg

Avocado Chocolate Mousse

1. **Prepare the Avocados (2 minutes)** Halve the avocados and remove the pits. Scoop the flesh into a blender. This is the base for the mousse, providing a creamy texture and healthy fats, crucial for achieving the desired consistency and nutritional profile.
2. **Add Cocoa and Sweetener (2 minutes)** Incorporate cocoa powder and sugar-free maple syrup or honey into the blender. These ingredients add the chocolate flavor and sweetness without increasing the sugar content, making the dessert suitable for diabetics.
3. **Blend with Liquid Ingredients (2 minutes)** Pour in the vanilla extract and almond milk. Blend until smooth. The liquid helps to process the mixture into a smooth mousse, with vanilla enhancing the flavor complexity.
4. **Season and Mix (2 minutes)** Add a pinch of salt to the blender and pulse to combine. Salt balances the sweetness and brings out the chocolate flavor, providing depth to the mousse.
5. **Chill and Serve (2 minutes)** Divide the mousse into serving dishes and refrigerate for a few minutes before serving. This step allows the mousse to set slightly, enhancing its texture and flavor, making it a refreshing dessert.

INGREDIENTS

- 2 medium (300g) Ripe avocados
- 1/4 cup (30g) Unsweetened cocoa powder
- 2 tablespoons (30ml) Sugar-free maple syrup or honey
- 1 teaspoon (5ml) Vanilla extract
- 2 tablespoons (30ml) Almond milk (or any milk of choice)
- A pinch (0.5g) Salt

NUTRITION

- **Kcal:** 250 Kcal
- **Carbohydrates:** 18g
- **Sugars:** 1g (natural sugars from avocado and sugar-free sweeteners)
- **Fiber:** 7g
- **Protein:** 4g
- **Total Fats:** 20g
- **Saturated Fats:** 3g
- **Monounsaturated Fats:** 10g
- **Polyunsaturated Fats:** 3g
- **Sodium:** 150mg

WEEK 1

Monday
- **Breakfast:** Scrambled Eggs with Spinach and Feta
- **Snack:** Carrot and Cucumber Sticks with Hummus
- **Lunch:** Quinoa Salad with Cucumbers and Feta
- **Dinner:** Garlic Lemon Shrimp Over Zucchini Noodles

Tuesday
- **Breakfast:** Greek Yogurt with Mixed Berries and Flaxseeds
- **Snack:** Apple Slices with Peanut Butter (small serving)
- **Lunch:** Smoked Salmon and Avocado Salad
- **Dinner:** Pan-Seared Salmon with Spinach Salad

Wednesday
- **Breakfast:** Quick Oats with Almond Milk and Chia Seeds
- **Snack:** Mixed Nuts and Dried Fruit Trail Mix (small serving)
- **Lunch:** Turkey Breast and Avocado Lettuce Wraps
- **Dinner:** Chicken Fajitas with Pre-Cut Veggies

Thursday
- **Breakfast:** Almond Butter and Banana Smoothie (use half a banana to reduce sugar)
- **Snack:** Ricotta and Berry Whole Wheat Crackers
- **Lunch:** Greek Salad with Olives and Feta Cheese
- **Dinner:** Tofu and Vegetable Stir-Fry with Soy Sauce

Friday
- **Breakfast:** Mini Frittatas with Spinach and Feta
- **Snack:** Edamame Salad with Sesame Ginger Dressing
- **Lunch:** Caprese Salad with Balsamic Glaze
- **Dinner:** Spaghetti Squash with Marinara Sauce (Microwave Cooked)

Saturday
- **Breakfast:** Avocado Toast on Whole Grain Bread
- **Snack:** Cherry Tomatoes with Mozzarella Balls and Basil
- **Lunch:** Tuna Salad on Mixed Greens
- **Dinner:** Grilled Chicken Breast with Steamed Broccoli

Sunday
- **Breakfast:** Cottage Cheese with Pineapple Chunks (small serving for lower sugar)
- **Snack:** Fresh Fruit Salad with Mint (focus on low glycemic index fruits)
- **Lunch:** Vegan Tacos with Refried Beans and Avocado
- **Dinner:** Quick Beef Stir-Fry with Bell Peppers

WEEK 2

Monday
- **Breakfast:** Avocado Toast on Whole Grain Bread
- **Snack:** Steamed Green Beans with Lemon Zest
- **Lunch:** Smoked Salmon and Cream Cheese Cucumber Bites
- **Dinner:** Spicy Black Bean Soup

Tuesday
- **Breakfast:** Cottage Cheese with Pineapple Chunks
- **Snack:** Quick Pickled Cucumber Salad
- **Lunch:** Turkey and Cheese Roll-Ups
- **Dinner:** Pan-Seared Salmon with Spinach Salad

Wednesday
- **Breakfast:** Greek Yogurt with Honey and Cinnamon
- **Snack:** Sautéed Kale with Garlic and Olive Oil
- **Lunch:** Egg Salad on Whole Grain Toast
- **Dinner:** Vegan Tacos with Refried Beans and Avocado

Thursday
- **Breakfast:** Mini Frittatas with Spinach and Feta
- **Snack:** Tomato and Onion Salad with Olive Oil
- **Lunch:** Greek Salad with Olives and Feta Cheese
- **Dinner:** Garlic Lemon Shrimp Over Zucchini Noodles

Friday
- **Breakfast:** Quick Oats with Almond Milk and Chia Seeds
- **Snack:** Ricotta and Berry Whole Wheat Crackers
- **Lunch:** Tuna Salad on Mixed Greens
- **Dinner:** Shrimp and Avocado Taco Salad

Saturday
- **Breakfast:** Almond Butter and Banana Smoothie
- **Snack:** Mixed Nuts and Dried Fruit Trail Mix
- **Lunch:** Quinoa Salad with Cucumbers and Feta
- **Dinner:** Chicken Caesar Salad Wrap

Sunday
- **Breakfast:** Scrambled Eggs with Spinach and Feta
- **Snack:** Fresh Fruit Salad with Mint
- **Lunch:** Caprese Salad with Balsamic Glaze
- **Dinner:** Mango and Coconut Rice Paper Rolls

WEEK 3

Monday
- **Breakfast**: Cottage Cheese with Pineapple Chunks
- **Snack**: Apple Slices with Peanut Butter
- **Lunch**: Greek Salad with Olives and Feta Cheese
- **Dinner**: Garlic Lemon Shrimp Over Zucchini Noodles

Tuesday
- **Breakfast**: Almond Butter and Banana Smoothie
- **Snack**: Cherry Tomatoes with Mozzarella Balls and Basil
- **Lunch**: Tuna Salad on Mixed Greens
- **Dinner**: Chicken Fajitas with Pre-Cut Veggies

Wednesday
- **Breakfast**: Quick Oats with Almond Milk and Chia Seeds
- **Snack**: Ricotta and Berry Whole Wheat Crackers
- **Lunch**: Vegan Tacos with Refried Beans and Avocado
- **Dinner**: Pan-Seared Salmon with Spinach Salad

Thursday
- **Breakfast**: Greek Yogurt with Honey and Cinnamon
- **Snack**: Carrot and Cucumber Sticks with Hummus
- **Lunch**: Smoked Salmon and Cream Cheese Cucumber Bites
- **Dinner**: Spaghetti Squash with Marinara Sauce (Microwave Cooked)

Friday
- **Breakfast**: Scrambled Eggs with Spinach and Feta
- **Snack**: Fresh Fruit Salad with Mint
- **Lunch**: Caprese Salad with Balsamic Glaze
- **Dinner**: Quinoa Salad with Cucumbers and Feta

Saturday
- **Breakfast**: Avocado Toast on Whole Grain Bread
- **Snack**: Mixed Nuts and Dried Fruit Trail Mix
- **Lunch**: Turkey Breast and Avocado Lettuce Wraps
- **Dinner**: Tofu and Vegetable Stir-Fry with Soy Sauce

Sunday
- **Breakfast**: Mini Frittatas with Spinach and Feta
- **Snack**: Steamed Green Beans with Lemon Zest
- **Lunch**: Smoked Salmon and Avocado Salad
- **Dinner**: Grilled Chicken Breast with Steamed Broccoli

WEEK 4

Monday
- **Breakfast**: Dark Chocolate-Dipped Strawberries
- **Snack**: Edamame Salad with Sesame Ginger Dressing
- **Lunch**: Chicken Caesar Salad Wrap
- **Dinner**: Pork Tenderloin Medallions with Apple Slaw

Tuesday
- **Breakfast**: Greek Yogurt with Mixed Berries and Flaxseeds
- **Snack**: Quick Pickled Cucumber Salad
- **Lunch**: Vegan Pesto and Tomato Toast
- **Dinner**: Garlic Lemon Shrimp Over Zucchini Noodles

Wednesday
- **Breakfast**: Zucchini and Basil Soup
- **Snack**: Tomato and Onion Salad with Olive Oil
- **Lunch**: Turkey and Cheese Roll-Ups
- **Dinner**: Balsamic Glazed Steak Bites and Tomatoes

Thursday
- **Breakfast**: Pea and Mint Soup
- **Snack**: Cherry Tomatoes with Mozzarella Balls and Basil
- **Lunch**: Egg Salad on Whole Grain Toast
- **Dinner**: Shrimp and Avocado Taco Salad

Friday
- **Breakfast**: Avocado Chocolate Mousse
- **Snack**: Carrot and Cucumber Sticks with Hummus
- **Lunch**: Smoked Salmon and Cream Cheese Cucumber Bites
- **Dinner**: Quick Tomato Basil Soup

Saturday
- **Breakfast**: Ricotta and Honey with Sliced Almonds
- **Snack**: Berry and Nut Yogurt Parfait
- **Lunch**: Caprese Salad with Balsamic Glaze
- **Dinner**: Mango and Coconut Rice Paper Rolls

Sunday
- **Breakfast**: Frozen Blueberries with a Drizzle of Cream
- **Snack**: Mixed Nuts and Dried Fruit Trail Mix
- **Lunch**: Greek Salad with Olives and Feta Cheese
- **Dinner**: Chicken Caesar Salad Wrap

WEEK 5

Monday
- **Breakfast:** Greek Yogurt with Mixed Berries and Flaxseeds
- **Snack:** Apple Slices with Peanut Butter
- **Lunch:** Smoked Salmon and Avocado Salad
- **Dinner:** Quick Tomato Basil Soup

Tuesday
- **Breakfast:** Dark Chocolate-Dipped Strawberries
- **Snack:** Carrot and Cucumber Sticks with Hummus
- **Lunch:** Chicken Fajitas with Pre-Cut Veggies
- **Dinner:** Tofu and Vegetable Stir-Fry with Soy Sauce

Wednesday
- **Breakfast:** Frozen Blueberries with a Drizzle of Cream
- **Snack:** Cherry Tomatoes with Mozzarella Balls and Basil
- **Lunch:** Spinach and Goat Cheese Stuffed Portobello Mushroom
- **Dinner:** Pork Tenderloin Medallions with Apple Slaw

Thursday
- **Breakfast:** Ricotta and Honey with Sliced Almonds
- **Snack:** Berry and Nut Yogurt Parfait
- **Lunch:** Vegan Pesto and Tomato Toast
- **Dinner:** Spaghetti Squash with Marinara Sauce

Friday
- **Breakfast:** Zucchini and Basil Soup
- **Snack:** Edamame Salad with Sesame Ginger Dressing
- **Lunch:** Avocado and Black Bean Salad
- **Dinner:** Grilled Chicken Breast with Steamed Broccoli

Saturday
- **Breakfast:** Pea and Mint Soup
- **Snack:** Roasted Red Pepper and Walnut Dip
- **Lunch:** Simple Miso Soup
- **Dinner:** Balsamic Glazed Steak Bites and Tomatoes

Sunday
- **Breakfast:** Avocado Chocolate Mousse
- **Snack:** Cauliflower Fried Rice with Egg and Peas
- **Lunch:** Zucchini and Corn Sauté with Basil
- **Dinner:** Quick Veggie and Hummus Sandwich

WEEK 6

Monday
- **Breakfast:** Greek Yogurt with Honey and Cinnamon
- **Snack:** Cherry Tomatoes with Mozzarella Balls and Basil
- **Lunch:** Smoked Salmon and Cream Cheese Cucumber Bites
- **Dinner:** Quinoa Salad with Cucumbers and Feta

Tuesday
- **Breakfast:** Scrambled Eggs with Spinach and Feta
- **Snack:** Apple Slices with Peanut Butter
- **Lunch:** Tuna Salad on Mixed Greens
- **Dinner:** Grilled Chicken Breast with Steamed Broccoli

Wednesday
- **Breakfast:** Cottage Cheese with Pineapple Chunks
- **Snack:** Edamame Salad with Sesame Ginger Dressing
- **Lunch:** Vegan Tacos with Refried Beans and Avocado
- **Dinner:** Garlic Lemon Shrimp Over Zucchini Noodles

Thursday
- **Breakfast:** Almond Butter and Banana Smoothie
- **Snack:** Carrot and Cucumber Sticks with Hummus
- **Lunch:** Turkey Breast and Avocado Lettuce Wraps
- **Dinner:** Chicken Caesar Salad Wrap

Friday
- **Breakfast:** Quick Oats with Almond Milk and Chia Seeds
- **Snack:** Mixed Nuts and Dried Fruit Trail Mix
- **Lunch:** Caprese Salad with Balsamic Glaze
- **Dinner:** Pork Tenderloin Medallions with Apple Slaw

Saturday
- **Breakfast:** Mini Frittatas with Spinach and Feta
- **Snack:** Fresh Fruit Salad with Mint
- **Lunch:** Greek Salad with Olives and Feta Cheese
- **Dinner:** Spaghetti Squash with Marinara Sauce

Sunday
- **Breakfast:** Avocado Toast on Whole Grain Bread
- **Snack:** Ricotta and Berry Whole Wheat Crackers
- **Lunch:** Smoked Salmon and Avocado Salad
- **Dinner:** Mango and Coconut Rice Paper Rolls

WEEK 7

Monday
- **Breakfast:** Greek Yogurt with Honey and Cinnamon
- **Snack:** Apple Slices with Peanut Butter
- **Lunch:** Quinoa Salad with Cucumbers and Feta
- **Dinner:** Grilled Chicken Breast with Steamed Broccoli

Tuesday
- **Breakfast:** Cottage Cheese with Pineapple Chunks
- **Snack:** Carrot and Cucumber Sticks with Hummus
- **Lunch:** Turkey Breast and Avocado Lettuce Wraps
- **Dinner:** Garlic Lemon Shrimp Over Zucchini Noodles

Wednesday
- **Breakfast:** Scrambled Eggs with Spinach and Feta
- **Snack:** Fresh Fruit Salad with Mint
- **Lunch:** Caprese Salad with Balsamic Glaze
- **Dinner:** Balsamic Glazed Steak Bites and Tomatoes

Thursday
- **Breakfast:** Avocado Toast on Whole Grain Bread
- **Snack:** Mixed Nuts and Dried Fruit Trail Mix
- **Lunch:** Vegan Tacos with Refried Beans and Avocado
- **Dinner:** Pan-Seared Salmon with Spinach Salad

Friday
- **Breakfast:** Almond Butter and Banana Smoothie
- **Snack:** Cherry Tomatoes with Mozzarella Balls and Basil
- **Lunch:** Smoked Salmon and Avocado Salad
- **Dinner:** Tofu and Vegetable Stir-Fry with Soy Sauce

Saturday
- **Breakfast:** Quick Oats with Almond Milk and Chia Seeds
- **Snack:** Edamame Salad with Sesame Ginger Dressing
- **Lunch:** Chicken Caesar Salad Wrap
- **Dinner:** Pork Tenderloin Medallions with Apple Slaw

Sunday
- **Breakfast:** Mini Frittatas with Spinach and Feta
- **Snack:** Ricotta and Berry Whole Wheat Crackers
- **Lunch:** Greek Salad with Olives and Feta Cheese
- **Dinner:** Spaghetti Squash with Marinara Sauce (Microwave Cooked)

WEEK 8

Monday
- **Breakfast:** Ricotta and Honey with Sliced Almonds
- **Snack:** Steamed Green Beans with Lemon Zest
- **Lunch:** Smoked Salmon and Avocado Salad
- **Dinner:** Quick Beef Stir-Fry with Bell Peppers

Tuesday
- **Breakfast:** Mango and Coconut Rice Paper Rolls
- **Snack:** Roasted Red Pepper and Walnut Dip with Vegetable Sticks
- **Lunch:** Turkey and Cheese Roll-Ups
- **Dinner:** Garlic and Herb Microwave-Steamed Carrots with Grilled Chicken

Wednesday
- **Breakfast:** Quick Tomato Basil Soup (served chilled or warm depending on preference)
- **Snack:** Fresh Fruit Salad with Mint
- **Lunch:** Vegan Pesto and Tomato Toast
- **Dinner:** Shrimp and Corn Soup

Thursday
- **Breakfast:** Zucchini and Basil Soup
- **Snack:** Cherry Tomatoes with Mozzarella Balls and Basil
- **Lunch:** Chicken Caesar Salad Wrap
- **Dinner:** Spaghetti Squash with Marinara Sauce (Microwave Cooked)

Friday
- **Breakfast:** Pea and Mint Soup
- **Snack:** Mixed Nuts and Dried Fruit Trail Mix (in moderation)
- **Lunch:** Caprese Salad with Balsamic Glaze
- **Dinner:** Pan-Seared Salmon with Spinach Salad

Saturday
- **Breakfast:** Dark Chocolate-Dipped Strawberries (small portion)
- **Snack:** Apple Slices with Peanut Butter
- **Lunch:** Greek Salad with Olives and Feta Cheese
- **Dinner:** Tofu and Vegetable Stir-Fry with Soy Sauce

Sunday
- **Breakfast:** Cottage Cheese with Pineapple Chunks
- **Snack:** Carrot and Cucumber Sticks with Hummus
- **Lunch:** Smoked Salmon and Cream Cheese Cucumber Bites
- **Dinner:** Grilled Chicken Breast with Steamed Broccoli and Quick Pickled Cucumber Salad

Printed in Great Britain
by Amazon